100 Greatest 70s

The Stories Behind the Pop Music of the 1970s

Frank Mastropolo

100 Greatest 70s Pop Songs
The Stories Behind Pop Music of the 1970s

Frank Mastropolo

© 2025 Frank Mastropolo

All rights reserved. No part of this work may be reproduced or used in any form or by any means—graphic, electronic, or mechanical, including photocopying or information storage and retrieval systems—without written permission from the author.

The scanning, uploading, and distribution of this book or any part thereof via the Internet or any other means without the permission of the publisher is illegal and punishable by law. Please purchase only authorized editions and do not participate in or encourage the electronic piracy of copyrighted materials.

Art Director: Pete Mastropolo
Researcher: Beverly Mastropolo

Cover Design: Pete Mastropolo

ISBN: 979-8-89692-638-2
eISBN: 979-8-89692-636-8

Published by Edgar Street Books® New York

"Afternoon Delight" by the Starland Vocal Band

Bill Danoff and his then-wife Taffy were a struggling folk duo known as Bill and Taffy in 1974. The Danoffs recorded two albums for RCA Records that failed to sell. Bill thought their fortunes might change as a vocal group by adding vocalist Jon Carroll and Margot Chapman.

"I wasn't really looking to put a group together," Bill told Melody Maker, "but I just thought that if we were going to have a group, it would be a good idea to have the four of us.

"I was thinking about the vocal idea, how we all got along, and how it would work."

Signed by John Denver's Windsong Records, the Starland Vocal Band released "Afternoon Delight" in 1976. The song's sly references to afternoon sex helped it top the Billboard chart.

Bill got the inspiration for the song in 1974 when he and Chapman stopped for lunch at Clyde's, a Washington, DC bar.

"It was after lunch," Bill told the Washington Post, "and from three to six they had these table tents out that said 'Afternoon Delights.' It was a little menu of like four items. I thought it would be a neat title for a song."

"I didn't want to write an all-out sex song," Bill told the Los Angeles Times. 'I just wanted to write something that was fun and hinted at sex."

"All by Myself" by Eric Carmen

Eric Carmen was the lead vocalist of the Raspberries, whose biggest hit was 1972's "Go All the Way." Carmen embarked on a solo career in 1975 after the breakup of the Raspberries. The first single of his 1975 self-titled debut album was "All by Myself."

"The Raspberries were on Capitol, and after 'Go All the Way,' all Capitol wanted to know from us was 'Son of Go All the Way,'" Carmen explained in Pop Matters.

"Give us another 'Go All the Way.' And we had a lot more that we could do besides just 'Go All the Way.'

"So when I went to Arista, I had a period of writing where I suddenly was unrestricted. I wasn't writing for a band for the first time. It opened up a whole other arena for me to work within."

Carmen explained on his website how he wrote "All by Myself."

"The song started with the solo," said Carmen. "It started four bars at a time. Eventually, over a period of two months, that entire interlude had been written.

"Then my quest was to put this in the middle of an actual song. Then it was a matter of trying to figure out what kind of song and how could I do it. I was listening to Rachmaninoff's second piano concerto, and I heard the melody, which I used for the verse.

"Then I needed a chorus. I went back and listened to a song that I had written in 1973 called 'Let's Pretend' for the Raspberries. I thought, 'Let's Pretend' was a nice melody. The song didn't go quite as far as I thought it should have. I'll go back and steal from myself for this.'"

"Clive Davis decided that 'All by Myself' should be the first single, and I agreed with him. I wanted it to be a radical departure from the Raspberries. I didn't want it to be just, like, 'Here's Eric, and he's a continuation of what he did.'"

"All by Myself" was Carmen's biggest hit, reaching No. 2 in 1976. Carmen believed no copyright existed on Rachmaninoff's music because it was in the public domain in the US. However, the music was protected internationally.

When he was notified, Carmen agreed that the Rachmaninoff estate would receive 12 percent of the royalties from "All by Myself."

"Angie Baby" by Helen Reddy

"Angie Baby" is the enigmatic song by Helen Reddy that topped the charts in 1974. Australian songwriter Alan O'Day explained in Forgotten Hits how he wrote the song about a young girl who "lives life in the songs."

"Back in 1974, I was trying to write a song loosely based on the character in the Beatles' 'Lady Madonna,'" said O'Day. "My thoughts went back several years to a young next-door neighbor girl. Very quiet, kept to herself. Although I hardly knew her, I liked to imagine what she thought about.

"Mentally, she lived in a dream world of lovers inspired by the songs on her radio. Thus, she appeared to be completely vulnerable to the prurient interests of her male neighbor.

"As the lyric progresses, we assume that the evil-minded neighbor will have his way with her. But that's where the twist comes in: as he enters her world, i.e., her bedroom, it becomes a reality for him as well, with weird and unexpected consequences."

"If I were going to teach a course on songwriting," Reddy told Billboard, "I think I'd use 'Angie Baby' as my textbook."

"I think 'Angie Baby' is powerful," O'Day told The Muse's Muse, "because it plays with fantasy and reality, relates an unexpected shift in power, questions the distinction between insanity and magic, and takes the listener on a wonderful ride."

"Annie's Song" by John Denver

John Denver wrote "Annie's Song" about Ann Martell, his college sweetheart, whom he married in 1967. The tune topped the charts in 1974.

"Annie's Song" was written after a ski run on Aspen Mountain in Colorado. "It was written after John and I had gone through a pretty intense time together and things were pretty good for us," Martell recalled.

"He left to go skiing, and he got on the Ajax chair on Aspen Mountain, and the song just came to him. He skied down and came home, and wrote it down.

"Initially it was a love song and it was given to me through him, and yet for him it became a bit like a prayer."

"Suddenly, I'm hypersensitive to how beautiful everything is," Denver wrote in Take Me Home: An Autobiography.

"All of these things filled up my senses, and when I said this to myself, unbidden images came one after the other. All of the pictures merged, and I was left with Annie. That song was the embodiment of the love I felt at that time."

"Baby Don't Get Hooked on Me" by Mac Davis

By 1972, singer-songwriter Mac Davis had written hits for Elvis Presley ("Suspicious Minds"), Bobby Goldsboro ("Honey"), and Kenny Rogers ("Lady") but had yet to score a hit of his own. Producer Rick Hall chided Davis to record a song with a hook, a memorable phrase that catches the listener's ear.

"I was recording at the FAME Studio in Muscle Shoals, Alabama, with Rick Hall producing," Davis told Songwriter Universe.

"He kept bugging me, saying, 'You know, you've got to give me a hook, man, you gotta give me a hook song. I can't get hits with these old, syrupy love ballads you're bringing in.

"'You give all your hook songs to Elvis, Bobby Goldsboro, and Kenny Rogers, and then you bring me these old love ballads. I need a hook!'

"So as a joke, while he was adding musicians to a track, I went up to his office and I stole a yellow legal pad. Then, I got a bottle of his scotch and set it on his desk, and I was just fiddlin' around, and I ended up writing the hook for the song.

"I came up with 'Baby, baby, don't get *hooked* on me'—wink wink. Then I went back downstairs and I stopped everything—I was winking to the musicians there.

"I said to Rick, 'I think I got you a hook song.' I sang, 'Baby, baby don't get hooked on me." And by the time I got through the chorus, he says, 'That's a smash.' I said to him, 'You didn't get the joke: Hooked on me.'

"He said, 'I don't care what it is. It's a smash and we're gonna cut it.'"

"Baby Don't Get Hooked on Me" was indeed a smash for Davis, topping the charts in 1972.

"I thought it was a little bit chauvinistic," Davis said in American Songwriter. "In fact, it became Ms. Magazine's chauvinist pig song of the year for 1972. I used to tell everybody, 'Thank God Paul Anka came up with "You're Having My Baby" and took it away from me.'"

"Bad Blood" by Neil Sedaka

"Bad Blood" was a No. 1 hit in 1975, part of Neil Sedaka's career resurgence that came after signing with Elton John's Rocket Records. John performed uncredited backing vocals on "Bad Blood," which ensured airplay.

"Bad Blood" was written by Sedaka and Philip Cody, who explained its inspiration in Songfacts.

"I spent some time with my grandmother, who is an old Sicilian lady. She was telling stories about the lady up the street who used to be a witch, a Strega. And the whole idea of people being good or evil because of what goes on in their blood was just part of the superstitious nature of my Sicilian upbringing that I tried to stay as far away from as I could [*laughs*].

"I just thought it would be an interesting way to approach a lyric; rather than from a place of enlightenment, the idea is that love makes us stupid."

The song's references to the woman who dumped Sedaka as "the bitch" and "an evil child" ran counter to his catalog of feel-good tunes like "Breaking Up Is Hard to Do" and "Calendar Girl."

"The lyric is a little controversial, with words like 'bitch' and such," Sedaka told Rolling Stone. "I like it because it's not such a goody-goody two-shoes thing.

"That's the mistake I made in my first career—the songs were too predictable, there's no message intended."

"Band of Gold" by Freda Payne

Motown's songwriting and producing team Holland-Dozier-Holland were embroiled in a lawsuit with the Detroit label when they wrote "Band of Gold." They were sued by

Motown when they left to form their own labels, Invictus and Hot Wax.

"Brian and Eddie Holland and I had written and produced huge hits for the likes of the Supremes and the Four Tops, and felt we deserved our own offshoot label," Lamont Dozier explained in The Guardian.

"But Berry Gordy, Motown's boss, wouldn't allow it. We went ahead anyway, setting up Invictus and Hot Wax in 1969. People said, 'If Holland-Dozier-Holland have left, that's the end of Motown.' So Berry sued us, and we sued him back. It was a very unhappy time.

"'Band of Gold' was one of the first Invictus singles. Because we were contracted to Motown and were in court, we could only produce songs, not write them. So it's credited 'R Dunbar – E Wayne.'

"Ron Dunbar was in our A&R department; Edythe Wayne also worked at the company. Neither were writers—we just had to put somebody's name on the thing!

"Everyone knew it was really Holland-Dozier-Holland. Brian and I would come up with the tunes on the piano. I'd also do titles and themes, while Eddie would turn them into lyrics.

"Freda Payne was our first choice as singer. We'd all been at school together. She had a great voice, perfect for this—and she didn't have a recording contract."

"In the studio, it was like being with three friends, although they were very professional and wanted things done a certain way," said Payne.

"Not everybody who signed to Invictus became successful, but in the studio, I had a premonition. I said, 'I have a feeling I'm going to come out on top.' We all had something to prove.

"When I first heard 'Band of Gold,' I was in my 20s and thought it was written for a teenager to sing, a 16-year-old who's just got married too young. My reading was that she was frigid or scared and didn't know what to do in the bedroom, but Ron Dunbar said, 'You don't have to like it—just sing it!'"

Dozier told Songfacts that the writers had a different interpretation of the lyrics. "The story was, the girl found out this guy was not all there," said Dozier.

"He had his own feelings about giving his all. He wanted to love this girl; he married the girl, but he couldn't perform on his wedding night because he had other issues about his sexuality. I'll put it that way.

"It was about this guy that was basically gay, and he couldn't perform. He loved her, but he couldn't do what he was supposed to do as a groom, as her new husband. I know it sounds simple, but that's where the idea came from."

"Band of Gold" was a No. 3 smash in 1970, the only Top 10 hit of Payne's career.

"Beach Baby" by the First Class

Vocalist Tony Burrows was asked by John Carter, his former bandmate in the group Ivy League, to sing lead on a song he'd written with his wife, Jill Shakespeare. "He called me and told me he had a song he wanted me to do and said, 'I've got a feeling about this demo,'" Burrows told Rebeat.

"The demo was just John and a guitar, and he was singing the song, but I could tell there was something there.

"So we went into the studio and recorded it. There were basically about 18 different tracks, and John and I did all of the backing vocals as well as the lead."

In 1974, "Beach Baby" reached No. 4, the only hit the First Class would have.

"I heard that when Brian Wilson first heard 'Beach Baby,' he said, 'I don't know who it is, but it's definitely West Coast America,'" recalled Burrows. 'Which I took as a great, great tribute—I really did.

"I grew up with American pop music. We had recorded it as basically a tribute to the Beach Boys. I've since met him two or three times, and the other guys as well, and I've heard that when people are going into the theater for one of his shows, he often plays 'Beach Baby,' which is really nice."

"Born to Be Alive" by Patrick Hernandez

French singer Patrick Hernandez told France Net Infos that he intended the title of "Born to Be Alive" to be a pleonasm: the use of more words than necessary as emphasis (e.g., "repeat again") to convey meaning.

"I wrote this song for somewhat special reasons," said Hernandez. "Its title could pass for a pleonasm, albeit one that opened rather nice doors.

"I saw people around me living half their life, and not concretely, and that's not in my character. Hence, this was a kind of reaction to this inertia of those around me.

"The word 'alive' appealed to me."

Hernandez recorded "Born to Be Alive" in 1975 with his band Paris Palace Hotel. "I wrote 'Born to Be Alive' four years ago," Hernandez said on American Bandstand in 1979, "and it was a rock and roll version, and now it's disco.

"I decided to change the style one year ago when I came back to show business. I left show business for a year and moved to the French countryside."

"Born to Be Alive" topped the disco chart in 1979 and became a crossover No. 16 hit on the pop chart. Its success led Hernandez to hire dancers for his upcoming tour. One of the dancers went on to become a superstar.

"In July 1979, the success of 'Born to Be Alive' was global," Hernandez told Paris Match. "I'm in New York with the production team for auditions.

"We are looking for dancers and singers to surround me during the concerts of an American tour. Then up steps this young girl who impresses us all. This is Louise Ciccone, not yet Madonna, 19 years old. I am blown away by her performance; it was original and marked by a strong personality."

Madonna spent three months with Hernandez before returning to New York to pursue her music career.

"She knew exactly what she wanted and was never accepting any compromise," Hernandez said in OK magazine. "She was a diva even before becoming a star."

"Brand New Key" by Melanie

Melanie Safka had the biggest hit of her career with "Brand New Key," a tune that topped the charts in 1972. "Brand New Key" was produced by Melanie's husband, Peter Schekeryk, and was released on her 1971 album Gather Me. Melanie explained the inspiration for the song in Examiner.com.

"I was fasting with a 27-day fast on water. I broke the fast and went back to my life living in New Jersey, and we were going to a flea market around six in the morning. On the way back from the flea market, we passed a McDonald's, and the aroma hit me, and I had been a vegetarian before the fast.

"So we pulled into the McDonald's and I got the whole works, the burger, the shake, and the fries, and no sooner after I finished that last bite of my burger, that song was in my head.

"The aroma brought back memories of roller skating and learning to ride a bike, and the vision of my dad holding the back fender of the tire. And me saying to my dad, 'You're holding, you're holding, you're holding, right?' Then I'd look back and he wasn't holding, and I'd fall. So that whole thing came back to me and came out in this song."

Some radio stations banned "Brand New Key" on the assumption that the key and the lock in the lyrics had sexual connotations. Melanie went through a period of hating the song.

"I guess a key and a lock have always been Freudian symbols, and pretty obvious ones at that," Melanie told Super Seventies.

"There was no deep, serious expression behind the song, but people read things into it. They made up incredible stories as to what the lyrics said and what the song meant."

"When I first wrote it, it was like a slow ditty," Melanie told Best Classic Bands in 2018, "and my husband said no, we're going to speed it up and maybe add a background vocal part, syncopated and percussive."

"He was a genius in the studio, and he made it a hit record, and I was angry with him for doing that. How could you do this to me?

"And of course, coupled with pushing me as the silly non-relevant person, it worked, the perfect, silly, cute song. We went in the studio. We did it, and it was speeded up and we recorded it and it became a hit.

"I became a reactionary to it. I hated it. I didn't want to do it. I didn't want it to be my hit record. I didn't want it to be the song that people knew. But now I love it.

"What an amazing production, and it's timeless. It has the vintage thing. I love the song. I love that I wrote it. I love that it was a hit. It meant a lot to a lot of people, and I understand. It's not my finest poetry. It's a cute song."

"Count on Me" by Jefferson Starship

Jefferson Starship was formed by members of the psychedelic rock band Jefferson Airplane in 1974. By 1978, the band's music became softer and more melodic.

Starship's 1978 album, Earth, included "Count on Me," a No. 8 hit. Its use of strings led bassist and keyboardist David Freiberg to call it "the wimpy end of the stick" in Guitar Player.

"We're just passing out of the Seventies, which is like a big sleep after the Sixties," countered rhythm guitarist Paul Kantner in Rolling Stone.

"It's a light time, and the album feels real good to me on a light level—not the same way, but the good aspects, if you will, of disco. Just the feel—the bubbling level. I don't think every album has to be serious and heavy."

Marty Balin performed lead vocals on "Count on Me." "I have a friend named Jesse Barish—he's the most prolific songwriter I've ever seen," Balin told Best Classic Bands.

"He writes lots of great songs, and I did some of his songs. He wrote "Count on Me" and my solo hits "Hearts" and "Atlanta Lady." And sometimes when I would play with my own band, when Starship wasn't on tour, I would go out and play with local bands and local guys, and I'd sing some of those songs."

"That was probably the only acoustic solo I ever did before I started doing my solo stuff," guitarist Craig Chaquico said in Something Else Reviews.

"I remember being in Safeway in the checkout line, and 'Count on Me' came on the sound system. That's almost like hearing yourself in the elevator!

"It's kind of cool because you've made it into the pop culture; you're part of that lexicon now. They can play you in Safeway, along with Barry Manilow or something. I'm not saying that in a bad way, it's just a different way of hearing yourself.

"This was about 20 years ago, and I was patting myself on the back, standing in line at Safeway. I had just left Starship and was about to get started on a first acoustic guitar record. It was like an omen, because this was one of the few times I had played that instrument back then.

"I hear the chorus leading up to the solo, and I'm all ready to savor every note of my acoustic guitar solo. It's just about ready to start, and I hear: 'Can we get a price check for broccoli in produce, please?'

"That's how important my acoustic solo was! It was not as important as the broccoli at Safeway. That was a reality check."

"Dance with Me" by Orleans

Orleans guitarist John Hall wrote "Dance with Me" with his then-wife Johanna. The song was Orleans' first Top 40 hit, reaching No. 6 for the soft rock band in 1975.

"I was sitting in the living room of the house that Johanna and I owned in Saugerties, NY, which is east of Woodstock," Hall said in Songwriter Universe.

"It was a Sunday morning, and I was playing guitar in the living room, fooling around with different tunings and progressions. Then I played that melody and Johanna called out, 'Sounds like 'Dance with Me.'

"So we started to write the song, and we came up with the lyrics for the first verse. But then it took two months before the song was finished.

"We were coming back from a gig in Ithaca, NY, and we were driving back to the Woodstock area. I was driving and she was the passenger, when suddenly she said, 'Pick the beat up and kick your feet up.' Then she started scribbling on the back of an envelope. By the time we got home, the song was finished."

"People may get confused because the lead vocals on the biggest hits, "Dance with Me" and "Still the One," for instance, were sung by Larry Hoppen, who had a legitimate tenor voice," Hall explained in Bands to Fans.

"I wrote those melodies and coached him through them, but I couldn't have sung those in those keys myself. But sometimes a guitar lick or a chord voicing will determine the best key for a song."

Hoppen told Classic Rock Bob that "Dance with Me" was not representative of the type of music Orleans liked to play.

"We were more of a rock, funky, college band," said Hoppen.

"And then 'Dance with Me' came out of the blue as an anomaly. But that's what broke through, and we got kind of pushed into the MOR (middle of the road) thing.

"We then toured with Melissa Manchester awhile—no shade on her—it was that kind of soft rock audience. We then toured with Little Feat, and that's where we belonged."

"Danny's Song"
by Loggins & Messina and Anne Murray

Singer-songwriter Kenny Loggins was a 17-year-old high school student when he wrote "Danny's Song" in 1966. The tune was a gift to his brother Dan on the birth of his first son, Colin.

"A lot of the lyric is taken, rephrased, from a letter my brother, Dan, wrote me when he and his wife, Sheila, were deciding to move to Berkeley just after their son, Colin, was born," Loggins told Rolling Stone.

"He talked about the baby, and that they were going to Berkeley with no money at all, starting fresh."

Loggins first recorded "Danny's Song" in 1970 with Gator Creek, a band comprised of studio musicians. Loggins teamed with Buffalo Springfield's Jim Messina and Loggins & Messina released "Danny's Song" on their debut album, Sittin' In.

While it failed to crack the Top 40, "Danny's Song" gained popularity from the frequent airplay it received on rock and adult contemporary radio stations.

Anne Murray released her cover of "Danny's Song" in 1972. It reached No. 7 in early 1973 and earned Murray a Grammy Award nomination for Best Female Pop Vocal Performance.

Loggins told Rock History Music that "Danny's Song" was the "first real song that I wrote. I always knew that that was an important song.

"My joke is that it always got me laid, which it did not. I was way too shy. But it served me well."

"Dark Lady" by Cher

"Dark Lady" became Cher's third No. 1 solo hit in 1974. The song tells the story of a woman who visits a fortune teller, a "dark lady" who advises her to break up with her boyfriend. When the woman learns that the fortune teller has slept with her boyfriend, she murders both of them.

"Dark Lady" was written by keyboardist Johnny Durrill while on tour with the Ventures. Durrill sent the unfinished lyrics to Cher's producer, Snuff Garrett, who had some definitive feedback.

"When I was on tour in Japan with the Ventures, I was writing an interesting song," Durrill recalled.

"I telegraphed the unfinished lyrics to Garrett. He said to 'make sure the bitch kills him.' Hence, in the song, both the lover and fortune teller were killed. That song became 'Dark Lady.'

"Everybody knew it was a hit the minute they heard Cher's vocal on the playback," said Durrill, "though she didn't particularly like it."

"At the time I was into Jackson Browne and Joni Mitchell and the Eagles, and those were the kinds of songs I wanted to do," Cher said in a 2015 interview with Billboard.

"I was doing these poppy songs. I was not content, necessarily, to do them. I never liked 'Dark Lady,' and it was a big hit.

"I was hanging around with Anjelica Huston, and Jack Nicholson, Warren Beatty, and I was singing 'Dark Lady.'"

They're making like fabulous art, and I'm making 'Dark Lady.'

"It's very kitschy, and it seemed to go along well with people's idea of who I was at that point. And I really wanted to do rock and roll. I wanted to do harder rock."

"'Dark Lady' was a pain in the ass because there was no place to take a breath," Cher told Vox. "There were so many words in that stupid song!"

"Disco Duck" by Rick Dees & His Cast of Idiots

By 1976, Rick Dees was a successful Memphis disk jockey, the morning man at WMPS-AM. Dees often dreamed up novelty songs for his radio show.

"I was working out in a gym in Memphis when disco was coming out, and I also worked in a club called Chesterfield's, telling jokes and spinning records," Dees told Billboard.

"The more I played the songs, the more I knew it might be time for a disco parody. One of the guys who worked out in the gym did a great duck voice, and I remembered a song called 'The Duck' by Jackie Lee back in the '60s, so I said, How about a Disco Duck?

"I had mice in my apartment at the time, and I went home and put my feet up on the chair, because nobody likes to have their feet dangling down if there might be a mouse nearby, and I wrote that song.

"It took me one afternoon. We went into the studio three months later—that's how long it took me to convince people to do the song."

Dees pitched the tune around Hollywood but got no takers until he played it for Al Coury, president of RSO Records.

"We talked to everybody in the business, and everybody passed on the song, except Al Coury," said Dees. "He said, 'Let me take it home and play it for my kids.'"

When Coury's children laughed, RSO released "Disco Duck," which became a surprise No. 1 hit in 1976.

Though the song became a national hit, Dees' radio station, WMPS, forbade Dees to play it. Competing stations in town wouldn't spin it either.

"Can you believe this?" Dees said on air. "I'm getting ready to go to California to appear on American Bandstand and The Midnight Special with a song I've written and performed called 'Disco Duck.' And this station isn't even playing it!"

That outburst got Dees fired by the station, but Dees got his revenge. Rival WHBQ hired Dees, who soon had the top morning show in Memphis.

"I didn't know anything about the record business," said Dees. "I just thought you put out a song, and it becomes a hit. Because of my being naive at the time, I thought it was gonna be a smash.

"Knowing what I know today, it's so hard to become number one. It takes a lot of luck and a lot of praying and a lot of good promotion people, plus a good song. I had no idea all those elements had to work in concert."

"Doesn't Somebody Want to Be Wanted" by the Partridge Family

"Doesn't Somebody Want to be Wanted" was one of a string of hits by the Partridge Family, the group of actors cast for the popular ABC sitcom that ran from 1970 to 1974. The tune reached No. 6 in 1971.

"Doesn't Somebody Want to be Wanted" was written by pop music pros Mike Appel, Jim Cretecos, and Wes Farrell. The song's most vocal critic was its lead singer, David Cassidy.

"Probably the thing that they had to twist my arm the hardest to do," Cassidy told Lost 45s, "was 'Doesn't Somebody Want to Be Wanted.'

"If you listen to the vocal, which is one of the worst vocal performances in the history of recording, in my opinion—it was with such restraint and they had me do that little talking bit in the middle, which is the most embarrassing moment in my entire career! I have never done that song since it was a hit live, and will never do it again!

"That one was a real difficult pill for me to swallow, because I really didn't like the song. What they did in the early days, which really used to drive me crazy, was they thought my voice was too husky and too powerful. They wanted me to sound younger.

"So what they would do is to slow the track down, and I would sing it and then they would bring it back to normal speed, so that I would sound even younger. They did that on that particular record, and I really hated it."

Cassidy revealed in his 1994 memoir C'mon Get Happy: Fear and Loathing on the Partridge Family Bus that his initial refusal to record the song brought a halt to the show's production.

After pressure from the studio, record company, and his management, Cassidy relented. He recorded "Doesn't Somebody Want to Be Wanted" but begged that it wouldn't be released.

"It was horrible, I was embarrassed by it," Cassidy wrote. "I still can't listen to that record."

"Don't Give Up on Us" by David Soul

David Soul's best-known role was Detective Kenneth "Hutch" Hutchinson in the 1970s TV series Starsky & Hutch. Soul, who had been a singer early in his career, recorded the No. 1 hit "Don't Give Up on Us" in 1977. The tune was written by Tony Macaulay, who penned "Baby Now That I've Found You" for the Foundations.

"I made an album in San Francisco for Private Stock, but there was nothing suitable for a single," Soul recalled in 1000 UK Number One Hits. "The company told me that Tony Macaulay had some good tunes, and he came over and played me 'Don't Give Up on Us' and 'Going in With My Eyes Wide Open.'

"Within 10 days, I had learnt the songs and recorded them, and Tony had mixed them and taken them back to England. They bazoomed to the top, and they are two songs which have stood the test of time."

Although he had several European hits in the 1970s, "Don't Give Up on Us" was Soul's only single to reach the Top 40 in the US.

"Don't Go Breaking My Heart" by Elton John & Kiki Dee

"Don't Go Breaking My Heart" marked a departure from the writing process for Elton John and Bernie Taupin. Usually, John would write lyrics after receiving music from Taupin. Producer Gus Dudgeon recalled on the Elton John website how the song took shape in a Toronto studio.

"Elton didn't have a lyric for it," said Dudgeon. "It was so weird to see him writing a song in the studio with no lyric. I'd never seen him do it before.

"And all he was singing was 'Don't go breaking my heart. Don't go breaking my heart. Don't go breaking my heart. Don't go breaking my heart. Don't go breaking my heart.' That's what he sang all the way through!"

"I was in Barbados one evening in 1976 when Elton called from Toronto to play me a backing track he'd just cut with the band," Taupin wrote in his autobiography Scattershot: Life, Music, Elton, and Me.

"Half cut myself by this point, the afternoon's poolside cocktails having muddied my brainwaves, I listened and took note. Elton was in need of a lyric that could be done as a duet. I told him I would give it a shot, hung up, and stuck my head in the ice bucket.

"In 10 minutes, I'd thrown something together that was simplistic without being overly trite, and that is how 'Don't Go Breaking My Heart' came about."

"Elton had produced my first album for Rocket, Loving and Free, in 1973, and we toured together in 1974," said Kiki Dee. "So perhaps when they came up with this song, they thought 'Well, it'd be nice to get Kiki on this' . . . 'cos I was in his life. It was pretty informal."

Dee was sent John's tracks from Toronto, and she recorded her vocals in London. "I remember getting a copy of it with Elton singing his vocal, and also doing my part in a high voice!

"I worked hard on my parts. Elton had already stamped the song with his vocal, which in a way is quite good, 'cos it gives you a groundwork on how you're gonna sing it. The precedent has already been set by him, and the writing and production of the song.

"I seem to remember working quite hard to get the right attitude. Good vocals are always hard work."

"Don't Go Breaking My Heart" topped the charts in 1976, John's sixth No. 1 single.

"I remember hearing it on the radio for the first time and thinking, 'Wow,'" said Dee. "'Cos some records, especially in those days, they have to sound great on the radio—and this was one of those records that did. I remember thinking, 'Oh, this could do okay—this could go.'"

"Don't It Make My Brown Eyes Blue" by Crystal Gayle

Crystal Gayle was a successful country singer in 1977 with three Top 10 country hits written by Richard Leigh. When Gayle's producer, Allen Reynolds, heard that Leigh could use some cheering up, he met with Leigh.

"We were sittin' on the floor singing songs to one another," Reynolds recalled in How Nashville Became Music City USA.

"Leigh mentioned a song that his publisher was gonna get to Shirley Bassey and sang it for me: 'Don't It Make My Brown Eyes Blue.' I said, 'Shirley Bassey, my ass, I want that song!'"

"When Alan heard the song, he said, 'You're not going to ship that song anywhere,' Gayle told Classic Bands. "He played it for me and I just loved it."

"Don't It Make My Brown Eyes Blue" was recorded at Jack's Tracks in Nashville in 1976.

"It was just one of those charmed sessions," said Reynolds. "After we presented the song to the musicians, it was about the third time running through that song that we ran tape.

"Gayle sang wonderfully. It came so fast that she wasn't sure that she had done her best job. I had to let her try to sing it again on two or three different occasions until she was comfortable with the original vocal take, and that's what we went with."

"It was a very first take in the studio," Gayle said. "When the red light went on and the machine turned on, that is what you hear, that went down that first time."

Hargus "Pig" Robbins played the song's signature piano riff. "Don't It Make My Brown Eyes Blue" was a crossover smash, reaching No. 1 on the country chart and No. 2 on the pop chart.

"What made it not go number one was 'You Light Up My Life,'" Gayle said with a laugh. "It was right on the tail of that one.

"It was just a song that I always say, says so much in so little. The emotion in the lyrics. It didn't have to be this long-winded song, if you understand what I'm talking about. It's just there with the emotion, with the melody, with what it says: 'Tell me no secrets. Tell me no lies.'"

"Do You Wanna Make Love" by Peter McCann

Singer-songwriter Peter McCann's "Do You Wanna Make Love" was a No. 5 hit in 1977. Its B-side, "Right Time of the Night," also written by McCann, was recorded by Jennifer Warnes and reached No. 6 that year. McCann told the Tennessean that he got the idea for the song at a famous Los Angeles club.

"'Do You Wanna Make Love' came out of a conversation I had with somebody at the Troubadour, at the bar there," said McCann.

"They were basically talking about the difference between one-night stands and being serious. So I wrote the song with those lines in it: 'Do you wanna make love / or do you just wanna fool around?'.

"A lot of people heard those first two lines, and they just thought it was a song about gratuitous, meaningless one-night stands. But the song was definitely not about that.

"There's a line in it, 'Take it seriously or take it somewhere else.' It's about this person really asking this person to take it seriously because the singer wants it to happen.

"Actually, I wrote 'Right Time of the Night' for a guy to sing, and I wrote 'Do You Wanna Make Love' for a woman to sing. Nobody was following that."

"Dueling Banjos" by Eric Weissberg and Steve Mandell

"Dueling Banjos" by Eric Weissberg and Steve Mandell gained popularity when it was used in the 1972 film Deliverance. Ronny Cox, a man from Atlanta, duels on acoustic guitar with Billy Redden, who plays a mentally challenged banjo player.

Weissberg, on banjo, and Mandell, on guitar, provided the track for the film. But "Dueling Banjos" has a history that goes back to the 1950s.

Arthur "Guitar Boogie" Smith wrote and recorded the song as "Feudin' Banjos," with Smith and Don Reno both playing banjos.

Bluegrass stars the Dillards were featured on the Andy Griffith Show in 1963 as the musical family the Darlings and played the song accompanied by Griffith.

Weissberg told Banjo News that director John Boorman heard the Dillards' version of Smith's tune and believed it was perfect for the scene. But Weissberg and Mandell were not Boorman's first choice to play it.

"This is the perfect example of being in the right place," said Weissberg. "Few people know this, but I wasn't the first call for playing 'Dueling Banjos.'

"At that time, the music department for Warner Bros. was headed by Joe Boyd. And Joe was from Cambridge, and was a close friend of Bill Keith, along with Jim Rooney, the Charles River Boys, and the Jug Band. And Joe, he of course calls Bill first, to do the gig, but Bill is in Germany, touring with the folk singer Karen Dalton, playing pedal steel, and he can't come back. So Bill suggests that Joe call me."

"Dueling Banjos" was a No. 2 hit in 1973. It won the Grammy Award for Best Country Instrumental Performance for Weissberg and Mandell. When Weissberg was credited as the arranger of "Dueling Banjos," Smith sued and won, receiving songwriting credit and royalties.

"I always hated 'Dueling Banjos,' because I had the original version, 'Feudin' Banjos,' with Arthur Smith and Don Reno," said Weissberg.

"I hated it because it wasn't bluegrass at all, it had a rhythm section, with drums. Who needs that?"

"Everything I Own" by Bread

Singer-songwriter David Gates wrote "Everything I Own," a No. 5 hit for Bread in 1972. Its lyrics seem to tell of an unrequited love, but Gates told The Guardian that it was a tribute to his late father.

"My father was kind and gentle and revered by everyone," said Gates. "He told me, 'People will do what you do, not what you say.' He always had time for me and taught me to read and write music, play various instruments, and introduced me to classical music, my foundation.

"One year, I sent my mom an orchid for her birthday, which I could scarcely afford. She was so touched—my dad wrote to tell me I could have had 'anything she owned' in return.

"My father died in 1963, and I wanted to write a song in memory of him. He did live to see some of my early progress towards success, but not the major songs or stardom with Bread. As with all my songs, the music led and the words tried to keep up, but they came pretty quickly.

"I wrote the lyrics 'I would give everything I own just to have you back again' so that they could be interpreted as a love song, but when I played it for my wife, she knew right away that it was about my father. She cried.

"The recording session with Bread felt pressurized because I wanted to convey the emotion in the vocal that existed when I played it with an acoustic guitar. 'Everything I Own' has reached farther than any other song I've ever written.

"Years after it was written, I started to reveal to audiences what it was about. The song is an opportunity to feel very strong emotions for the loss of time with someone you loved. I've been fortunate to watch it have such an impact on so many people."

"Fool (If You Think It's Over)" by Chris Rea

Chris Rea was a struggling British singer-songwriter when he recorded "Fool (If You Think It's Over)." The song was inspired by his younger sister Paula's heartbreak over the breakup with her first boyfriend.

Despite the song reaching No. 12 in 1978, Rea's biggest success in the US, the rock and blues guitarist hated the song. Rea was assigned to work with Gus Dudgeon, Elton John's producer, and their visions of the song clashed.

"I was never happy with that record," Rea said in Songfacts.

"Mainly, I did as I was told by a huge producer, and he'd been told by the record company to turn me into the next Elton John, which couldn't be further away from what I was.

"But they had decided that's what he was going to do. They didn't want me to sing low because that wasn't commercial.

"I've still got a piece of paper, and on the original lyrics it says: 'Fool (If You Think It's Over). Song for Al Green. 96 beats per minute. Al Jackson, drums.' And that's what 'Fool' was always meant to be."

"It never turned out the way I intended it to be," Rea told Jon Kutner. "I'd always seen it as a Memphis song and the trouble with it was that it was made a hit record so quickly, I never had the chance to voice my opinion about what I thought about the production and it still would have been a hit because it was hit song material but I'd always heard it as a Memphis tune."

Despite his protests, the song earned Rea a Grammy Award nomination as Best New Artist in 1979.

"It ended up being this huge California thing," Rea recalled in Classic Rock. "It's the only track I never played guitar on, which tells you something about the spirit of it. On top of that, it was just a huge hit. So there was nothing I could do. It was like, 'This is not me!'"

"Goodnight Tonight" by Wings

"Goodnight Tonight" was written and produced by Paul McCartney for his band Wings. The song was criticized by some rock critics for its disco style, but it was a No. 5 hit in 1979.

"That was all based round some rhythm," McCartney explained in Club Sandwich. "I do like dance records; when you listen to records, you're often down a club and want to dance with someone. I like dancin', actually!"

McCartney was inspired to write the song after a night at a disco. He recorded a demo of the track, playing all the instruments, and brought it to Wings in the studio.

Laurence Juber and Denny Laine played electric guitar, and Juber added the acoustic flamenco guitar that opens the song.

"Paul's recording was unfinished, so we did some work on it in January 1979 at Replica Studio in the basement of the MPL Soho office in London," Juber recalled in Paul McCartney: Recording Sessions (1969–2013).

"Denny and I did some electric parts echoing Paul's existing lead guitar. I don't remember who suggested the acoustic lead break, but the Spanish flavor was an obvious choice. I didn't have an acoustic guitar with me, so I used Denny's Ovation Adamas guitar—it was very quick, a one-take flamenco flourish!"

McCartney told Rolling Stone that "Goodnight Tonight" was almost not released.

"We had a meeting and decided it would be nice to have a single while the TV show, Wings Over America, was out, because it had been something like seven months since we'd put a record out.

"'Goodnight Tonight' was going to be the B-side and 'Daytime Nightime Suffering' was going to be the A-side. So we sat around years—well, it seemed like years—discussing it; you know, the normal soul-searching you go through. And we decided, 'No, it isn't all right; we won't put it out.'

"So we scrapped the whole thing. And about a week later, I played the record again. I thought, 'That's crazy, we've made it; it's stupid, why not put it out! Just because people are going to pan it.' I liked it, and other people had taken it home and played it to people at parties. So we decided to do it."

"Hold the Line" by Toto

"Hold the Line" was the first single from Toto's 1978 self-titled debut album. The song was written by keyboardist David Paich, who explained its inspiration in Songwriter Universe.

"I had left home for the first time and got an apartment," said Paich. "Then I got a Yamaha upright piano, and as soon as I started playing that piano, I started playing that riff.

"And I must have played it for two or three days, because people were knocking on my door saying, 'Stop playing!' I was annoying everybody by playing that song.

"It was around then that Toto decided to get together and have a rehearsal, listen to some new material, and see if we could actually be a band. So I brought that song in, and I taught it to singer Bobby Kimball, and Steve Lukather and Steven Hungate were there.

"And 'Hold the Line' sounded just like the record the first time we played it. So we knew we had a good thing.

"Hold the Line" became Toto's first hit, reaching No. 5 in 1978.

On the Toto website, drummer Jeff Porcaro said he emulated Greg Errico, the drummer of Sly & the Family

Stone, on the tune. Porcaro credited the funk rock pioneers for the song's vibe.

"'Hold the Line' was a perfect example of what people will describe as your heavy metal chord guitar licks, your great triplet A-notes on the piano, your 'Sly-Hot-Fun-in-the-Summertime' groove, all mishmashed together with a boy from New Orleans singing," said Porcaro.

"And it really crossed over a lot of lines."

"How Long" by Ace

"How Long" was a No. 3 hit for British band Ace in 1975. Singer Paul Carrack wrote the tune when the band was still struggling.

"My wife and I went to her mum's weekly visit where we got one square meal of the week," Carrack told Classic Bands.

"This I do remember, I wrote the lyric on the bus going to my future mother-in-law's. I wrote it on the back of that bus ticket. That's my excuse for there only being one verse."

Listeners often think "How Long" is about a cheating lover. Carrack explained its inspiration in Songwriter Universe.

"We were just a bar band," said Carrack. "We got together for fun to play in pubs and clubs across London. I had written this song, 'How Long,' which we were doing in our set.

"With 'How Long,' it's supposed to sound like a love song. But actually, it was about another band that was friends of ours, and they were trying to take our bass player. They were doing better than us, and they borrowed our bass player for a few shows.

"And unbeknownst to us, while he was in their camp, they were trying to persuade him to leave us and join them. We were this tight little band, we were great mates, and we loved our bass player, and it would have been a major blow if he joined this other band. But he didn't—he stuck with us and we got a song out of it [*laughs*]."

"I Can Help" by Billy Swan

Billy Swan wrote "Lover Please," a 1962 hit for Clyde McPhatter, but had yet to gain success as a solo artist when he moved to Nashville in 1973.

"When my wife and I got married, Kris Kristofferson and Rita Coolidge gave us a little RMI portable organ as a wedding present," Swan told the Elvis Australia fan club.

"Marlu fixed up a little music room in a little closet area of this duplex we were livin' in, and she had her little drum machine that went bom-bom-bom-bom," said Swan. "And I was playin' with that rhythm one time and started playin' the organ and that's when I wrote 'I Can Help.'"

"The song came in about 20 minutes," Swan said in Sound on Sound. "I didn't always write that quickly, but from my experience, the ones that come quickly are the good ones. 'Lover Please' was like that.

"With 'I Can Help,' I actually wrote the three verses first, and since I needed something to put between the second and third verse, I then came up with the bridge. The whole thing just came out of the air, including the words."

"I Can Help" topped the Billboard Pop and Country charts in 1974. The song was recorded with producer and engineer Chip Young at the Young 'Un Sound studio in Murfreesboro, TN.

"Chip set up a vocal mic, I stood in front of the organ, and what you hear was captured on the second take," said Swan.

"In fact, while I was playing the organ and singing, I was shaking my leg, and all through that second take, Chip's little puppy dog, a German Shepherd named Bowser, was pulling on my pants. That little thing wouldn't give up. It wasn't like he could pull me away or anything, but he was tugging on my leg all through what you hear on the record."

"I'd Like to Teach the World to Sing (In Perfect Harmony)" by the Hillside Singers and the New Seekers

"I'd Like to Teach the World to Sing (In Perfect Harmony)" began as a radio commercial jingle for Coca-Cola. The tune was based on "True Love and Apple Pie," a tune written by British songwriting team Roger Cook and Roger Greenaway and sung by Susan Shirley.

"In 1966, because the Fortunes had had such a big hit in America with 'You've Got Your Troubles,' I got a call from a guy called Bill Backer, who was the account executive for McCann Erickson on the Coca-Cola account in New York," Greenway told Songwriting magazine.

"In those days, if there was a hit group in the charts, they would hire them to sing Coca-Cola commercials. So we were asked to write a commercial for the Fortunes, which we did, and from that moment on—for literally the next five years—Roger Cook and I wrote dozens of Coke commercials for different acts.

"Then, around about 1970, we were commissioned to write a commercial for the New Seekers, which was going to be a two-minute radio ad for Coke. Normally, Roger and I would sit with Bill and a guy called Billy Davis, who was a producer at McCann Erickson, and we'd show them our ideas—unfinished songs—and then we'd finish them with whichever act we were working with."

Backer liked the melody of "True Love and Apple Pie," which was rewritten as "I'd Like to Teach the World to Sing."

"Then, about six months later—nearly a year after it was originally recorded—a guy called Harvey Gabor went to Bill Backer in the New York offices of McCann Erickson," said Greenaway.

"He always produced the TV commercials for Coca-Cola, and he said, 'I've got this idea for an ad with men and women standing on a hill, holding a bottle of Coke in their hands, singing an anthemic song. Is there anything you've recorded over the past few years that you think would fit the bill?'

"And Bill said, 'Look, there's a tape library with 10 years of music in there—why don't you go and listen?' So Harvey was in the library for three days, and eventually, he came out with a tape in his hand and said, 'I think I've found it, it's 'I'd Like to Teach the World to Sing' by the New Seekers.'"

When the TV commercial aired, Coca-Cola was deluged with calls and letters asking where the song could be bought. It prompted the creators to add three verses, remove the references to Coke, and release it as a single.

When the New Seekers balked at recording the song, a group of studio vocalists called themselves the Hillside Singers and assembled to record the tune, a No. 13 hit in 1972.

"We thought it was a silly, soppy song," New Singers' vocalist Lyn Paul told the Daily Mail. "So it was hilarious when they decided to make it into a single. I suppose it was a nice feel-good song, but seven million records! Even now I think, how did this very ordinary song ever do it?"

The song's success convinced the New Seekers to record their version, which reached No. 7.

"'Teach the World to Sing' would never have been a hit," said Greenaway, "had it not been for that wonderful idea that Harvey Gabor had of all the kids up on the hill with all the bottles of Coke in their hand."

"I'd Really Love to See You Tonight" by England Dan & John Ford Coley

England Dan Seals and John Ford Coley had a No. 2 hit in 1976 with "I'd Really Love to See You Tonight." The soft rock tune was the duo's first success. Coley explained in Rock Show Critique that they passed on the song when it was presented by their label, Big Tree Records.

"When they brought us 'I'd Really Love to See You Tonight,' we didn't want to do that song, we only wanted to do the songs that we had written, and that we were close to," said Coley.

"The unfortunate thing is that I think of all the songs that we had written, so far they had generated about $1.90 worth of sales, so when they brought it to us, we thought, 'Man, that's a woman's song. We don't really want to do it that way.' They said, 'No, try it. Try it. Just do it, and we can discuss all of that later.'

"So we did, and son of a gun, it took off the way that it did. The guy that wrote the song was Parker McGee, and I found myself at that point going, 'Hey, Parker, buddy, what else you got?'

"It was kind of a quick change when you recognized that there were other people that could actually write things that were going to get presented on the radio. Then you realized just how mercenary you can become.

"I love it when people say, 'Well, I won't compromise my music. I won't this, I won't that.' And you look at them now and go, 'I was one of those.' You look at them and go, 'Yeah, okay.'"

"I Go Crazy" by Paul Davis

With a full beard and hair down to his shoulders, Paul Davis did not fit the image of the 1970s singer-songwriter. His 1978 hit "I Go Crazy" reached No. 7 and spent 40 weeks on the Billboard Hot 100.

Davis told Classic Bands that people generally are surprised when they see him in person.

"I haven't had anybody freak out," said Davis. "I guess, overall, people are surprised, depending pretty much on whether I have my hair up or my hair down. Of course, a lot of people don't even know what I look like 'cause I've done very little road work."

Friend and producer Ed Seay told Vintage Rock that when Davis heard Lou Rawls' hit "You'll Never Find Another Love Like Mine," the singer decided to write a similar song for Rawls—until manager Ilene Berns stepped in.

"At that point, Paul was kind of frustrated at being a recording artist," recalled Seay. "He came over to my apartment and he played it on keyboard and it was great. Ilene, when she found out he wanted to give it to Lou Rawls, basically said, 'You ain't giving that to Lou Rawls! Get back there and make me a record!'"

Davis returned to the studio with producer Phil Benton and quickly reworked the demo Davis had recorded.

"Most of the time I have to work pretty hard at it," Davis said of his songwriting routine. "I don't write a lot of songs. Generally, I record everything I write.

"If I'm gonna cut ten songs, I don't have fifteen or sixteen songs to choose from. I'd be lucky if I have eight, because I take a long time to write. If I think of a ballad idea, I spend a lot of time on it."

And Lou Rawls? He recorded "I Go Crazy" in 1980.

"I Just Want to Be Your Everything" by Andy Gibb

Andy Gibb, the youngest of the Gibb brothers, scored a No. 1 hit out of the gate in 1977 with "I Just Want to Be Your Everything." The first single from Gibb's debut album, Flowing Rivers, was written by Barry Gibb.

"The first song we ever did, actually this was Barry, it wasn't me, was 'I Just Want to Be Your Everything,' which was done in Bermuda at Robert Stigwood's home, who managed both of us at the time," Gibb told Canadian DJ Bob Durant in 1985.

"That was my first contract. Robert became my manager, Barry was going to produce the record, he said, 'Let's go lock ourselves in a room, in a bedroom somewhere,' and when you're working with Barry, things go very fast. 'Cause he's an expert at his craft, you know, and within about 20 minutes he'd written a No. 1 record.

"Then we went right into another one; we co-wrote the next one, which is '(Love Is) Thicker Than Water.' That came in about 40, 50 minutes.

"(Love Is) Thicker Than Water" also topped the charts for Andy Gibb in 1977.

"It's just unbelievable when you are working with him. Not much of a story to tell on either song, because none of them are taken from any personal experiences; we just create a situation in our heads.

"It is something that only we know how it comes together. It is hard to explain it to somebody who isn't there, but we just don't draw on any old romance. We just create a situation and take it from there."

"I'll Never Fall in Love Again" by Dionne Warwick

In 1968, Broadway producer David Merrick asked lyricist Hal David and composer Burt Bacharach to write the score for his new musical, Promises, Promises. The songwriting team traveled with the cast during previews when Bacharach was stricken by pneumonia. That's when Merrick decided he needed a new song for the second act.

"I had just gotten out of the hospital," Bacharach told Record Collector. 'I'd been on the road and gotten pneumonia. We were on the road with Promises, Promises, and we'd try to get this song written and into the show the next night or two nights later.

"That's where Hal's line came from: 'What do you do when you kiss a girl, you get enough germs to catch pneumonia, after you do, she'll never phone ya.'

"So, having been in the hospital for five days with pneumonia, I got out and struggled to write that song, feeling not too great. You should take a rest after that and not go back into the Broadway show environment out on the road!"

"I wrote the melody for 'I'll Never Fall in Love Again' faster than I had ever written any song in my life," Bacharach wrote in Anyone Who Had a Heart: My Life and Music.

"We came in with the song the next morning, and it went into the show a couple of nights later. 'I'll Never Fall in Love Again' became the outstanding hit from the score and pretty much stopped the show every night."

Johnny Mathis was the first to chart with the tune in 1969. Bobbie Gentry had an international hit with "I'll Never Fall in Love Again" later that year. The most successful version was recorded by Dionne Warwick, who reached No. 6 in early 1970.

"I'm Easy" by Keith Carradine

Keith Carradine wrote and performed "I'm Easy" for the 1975 Robert Altman film Nashville. Carradine, as womanizing musician Tom Frank, performs the song to an audience of past, present, and possibly future lovers.

"There's a reason why Nashville is a lot of people's favorite Robert Altman film," Carradine told Ethan Alter. "It's an absolute masterwork that has stood the test of time and beyond.

"The 'I'm Easy' sequence was an example of Altman's loving cynicism at its best. I wrote that song as a straight-ahead love song with no double entendre. The fact that he put it in the context of the various liaisons my character had was his genius. It made for an unforgettable cinematic moment."

"I'm Easy" won the Academy Award for Best Original Song. Carradine recorded a single version of "I'm Easy" at a slightly higher tempo with added percussion, synthesizer, and keyboards, which was a Top 20 hit in 1976. Carradine explained in the AV Club that the record would have charted higher if it had been released as a single from the Nashville soundtrack album.

"It went up to No. 17 on the Billboard chart, and it probably would've made it to No. 1 if there hadn't been two versions of it in the marketplace," said Carradine.

"ABC Records, who had the soundtrack for Nashville, said, 'That's not a single, there's no way, it's not gonna get any airplay.' So we had the recording, but they didn't put it out!

"So I recorded another version of it for my own personal album that John Guerin produced under the aegis of David Geffen, who signed me to Asylum Records."

A Buffalo, NY radio station played the Nashville album cut and received a tremendous response.

"They played the song one day on the air, and they immediately got, like, 150 phone calls, people calling in and saying, 'What was that? I want to hear that again!'

"All of a sudden, it took off, and people were trying to buy it, but they couldn't, because ABC had not put it out there, and the Asylum version wasn't out yet.

"Then the thing won the Academy Award, and it was still a month after it won the Oscar before you could buy the single in a record store."

"It's Too Late" by Carole King

Carole King moved from New York to California's Laurel Canyon in 1968 after her divorce from songwriting partner Gerry Goffin. King and Goffin had written Brill Building classics, including "Will You Love Me Tomorrow" by the Shirelles.

King met Los Angeles painter and lyricist Toni Stern, and they co-wrote what's been called the ultimate break-up song, "It's Too Late."

"I'm sure there was a California quality in me that appealed to Carole," said Stern. "She was moving from a familial, middle-class lifestyle to Laurel Canyon, where she started to let her hair down, literally and figuratively. We worked off our contrasts."

"It's Too Late" was released as the B-side of "I Feel the Earth Move" from King's seminal 1971 album Tapestry. DJs soon flipped the record over, and "It's Too Late" topped the charts by May 1971.

"Toni Stern wrote the lyric to 'It's Too Late'—she handed it to me," King told Rolling Stone. "The music just came out of me.

"'Stayed in bed all morning just to pass the time / There's something wrong here, there can be no denying.' You can almost hear the music, or I could certainly, just by saying it. As I'm playing the piano, the music just came, and that song got written."

Stern told Sound Opinions that she often brought King lyrics written on a legal pad. "I wrote 'It's Too Late' in 20 minutes," said Stern. "She would take that pad, put it on the piano stand, and within an hour, hour and a half at the most, she would have the melody."

King revealed on CBS This Morning that she often hears from fans that "It's Too Late" helped get them through a breakup.

"Those lyrics are by Ms. Toni Stern," said King. "And her lyrics really do speak for people going through divorces."

"Junior's Farm" by Paul McCartney and Wings

"Junior's Farm" was written by Paul McCartney and recorded by his band, Wings. The roots of the 1974 No. 3 hit go back to McCartney's purchase of a Scottish estate called High Park Farm. In his memoir The Lyrics: 1956 to the Present, McCartney said the estate provided a respite from the business of being a Beatle.

"It was such a relief to get out of those business meetings with people in suits, who were so serious all the time," McCartney wrote, "and go off to Scotland and be able just to sit around in a T-shirt and corduroys. I was very much in that mindset when I wrote this song.

"The basic message is, let's get out of here. You might say it's my post-Beatles getting-out-of-town song."

To prepare for a 1974 US tour, McCartney needed a place to relax—and for Wings to rehearse. McCartney rented the Lebanon, TN home of Curly Putman, who wrote "Green, Green Grass of Home."

"We had two houses. One, the band, Wings, stayed in. I let them rent my place for six weeks for a pretty good little chunk of money," Putman told The Tennessean. "I won't say how much, because I can't remember, but it helped pay for my farm.

"And my son, Troy, he was about 14, 15, and my wife and I decided we'd go to Hawaii and let Paul McCartney pay for it.

"I had a double-car garage. That's where they set their band up and rehearsed. We got back from Hawaii, and I was anxious to get back home, of course.

"We were walking up the driveway, and they saw us coming, and Paul and the band started playing 'Green, Green Grass of Home.' It was an experience.

"Junior was me. I didn't know at first that he did this for me, but Claude Putman Jr. is my real name."

"'Junior's Farm' remains a good live song, and we usually put it in at the start of the set," McCartney wrote.

"It's got a lot of elements that work well—a recognizable introduction and a good steady rock and roll beat, and then these interesting, slightly surreal lyrics and a rousing chorus of 'Let's go, let's go.'

"That gets people in the mood to set out, 'just in the nick of time,' for their *own* version of 'Junior's Farm,' whatever that might be—wherever they want to disappear and hide out and just lie low."

"Just When I Needed You Most" by Randy VanWarmer

Singer-songwriter Randy VanWarmer's only hit was 1979's "Just When I Needed You Most." The heartfelt ballad was written by VanWarmer after he moved from Denver to Cornwall, England.

"Cornwall was kind of depressing," VanWarmer told Oblivioni. "The winters are long and very dark and rainy.

"I had a girlfriend from the States who came over and spent the summer with me and then went back to the States. So the song is about her, but the setting of Cornwall in the winter really provided the setting for the song.

"I'd been writing songs for a while and playing local folk clubs around Cornwall and South England, and I'd been taking tapes up to London around to various publishing companies. In those days, you could really just walk off the street even without an appointment, and somebody would listen to what you were doing."

VanWarmer signed a recording deal with Bearsville Records in London. Orchestral arranger Del Newman, who went on to work with Elton John and Rod Stewart, produced VanWarmer's debut album, Warmer.

"We cut the album in Nashville. 'Just When I Needed You Most' was one of the ten songs," said VanWarmer.

"We flew back to London, did the strings, finished the record, sent it to Warner Bros., which was the parent company. Then they shelved the record, and Bearsville Records pulled their offices out of London."

VanWarmer went to New York and lobbied Bearsville Records founder Albert Grossman to release the album in the US.

"I saw Albert and said, 'Is there any chance we could do something with the album?' and he said, 'Maybe we'll mix a couple songs and put out a single.' I picked 'Just When I Needed You Most.' I was just thinking this might be the only thing I get out, so at least I'll have it out. When we finally got the songs finished, Warner Bros. liked 'Just When I Needed You Most' and put it out."

"Just When I Needed You Most" was a No. 4 hit for VanWarmer in 1979. VanWarmer told The Item that the song's sorrowful message was its key to success.

"It's happened to everyone. That emotion is universal. I always hoped the record wasn't wallowing in self-pity and it had some redeeming value, and I guess it does."

"Knock Three Times" by Dawn

"Knock Three Times" was written by L. Russell Brown and Irwin Levine after producer Hank Medress requested a follow-up to Dawn's 1970 hit "Candida."

"I went to Irwin's house and Irwin said, 'Let's talk about how you grew up in the housing projects,'" Brown recalled in the Tennessean.

"I said, 'Well, we only had one phone in the building, but we had radiators with steam heat. And, if you lived on the second floor, someone with the phone would hit the radiator twice, bing, bing, and you would know the phone call was for you.

"Irwin said, 'I love that idea. Let's write a song about that.' So he created the title 'Knock Three Times,' and he wrote this lyric about a guy dreaming about a girl one floor below him. And he writes a string with a note and some insane kind of beautiful idea of a man dreaming of a girl, who just one floor below, he hears the music and he's envisioning everything.

"We took it into the producer, who asked us to write. He flipped out. I thought it was kind of like a 'teenybopper' song, because I was into the Doors. And I liked rock music, you know, and the Stones. I just thought it was a little cutesy, but I was playing, doing the best I could to keep the excitement up."

Medress asked Tony Orlando, who sang lead on "Candida," to record "Knock Three Times" for Bell Records.

Orlando had to disguise his identity as the lead singer of "Knock Three Times." Orlando was working as an executive for April-Blackwood Music, a subsidiary of Columbia Records.

Worried that recording for Bell was a conflict of interest with Columbia, Orlando insisted that "Candida" and "Knock Three Times" be credited to Dawn, a group that didn't exist. Orlando was reluctant to record the song at first.

"I said, 'Knock three times on the ceiling if you want me. Twice on the pipe if the answer is no—This song will only be a hit in Brooklyn,'" Orlando said in Goldmine.

"'In the Midwest, Hank, they don't have exposed pipes for steam heat. These are in tenement buildings. Okay. I will cut it for you because it won't be a hit.'"

When "Knock Three Times" reached No. 1 in January 1971, Orlando realized he had to tour to promote the record. He went to Columbia executive Clive Davis to explain.

"I finally went to Clive Davis and said, 'Clive, something has happened and I will need to leave the company.' He looked at me and said, 'Why, because you are Dawn?'

"I asked, 'Do you know this?' He replied, 'It is the worst-kept secret in show business. Of course, I know. I tell you what, Tony, this has been your dream since you were a little boy. You go find your dream, and you can always come home if it doesn't happen for you.'"

Telma Hopkins and Joyce Vincent were hired to tour with Orlando and continued to record hits as Tony Orlando and Dawn.

"Lady" by Styx

By 1975, Styx was at a crossroads. While popular in Chicago, they had recorded four albums without a national hit. "In those days, we were selling just enough for people not to lose money," singer-songwriter Dennis DeYoung recalled in Songwriter Universe.

"So they kept giving us money to go into the studio, and we kept making albums. But because the record company wasn't a real record company—it was a local company based in Chicago—we never got national exposure. And because of that, we could never get on a tour. We were stuck playing in Chicago all the time, where we were very popular."

"Lady," written by DeYoung, appeared on 1973's Styx II. "Lady" was written by DeYoung for his wife, Suzanne Feusi.

"Of all the chicks here on the South Side of the city of Chicago, where I grew up—it's not the most refined of areas," said DeYoung, "she has always carried herself with dignity and class—like a Lady. So yeah, it was written for Suzanne."

"Lady" was largely forgotten by 1975 when the band visited Chicago radio station WLS to promote their fourth album.

"The program director, Jim Smith, came out and said, 'Come on in.' We went in the conference room and we gave him our new album. He said, "I'm not going to play anything from this record. But starting tonight at eight o'clock, I'm going to play 'Lady' once a night at eight o'clock to see if it's a hit."

Smith's hunch was correct. "Lady" soon became a national hit, reaching No. 6 in March 1975.

"This guy, this program director Jim Smith, goes and picks 'Lady' out of thin air," DeYoung said on the Hardcore Humanism podcast. "I would have been done in music if 'Lady' hadn't been a hit.

"I look at it and I think, 'Wow! What a pivotal moment that that happened to me.' It's unbelievable to me, when I look back on it, how close we were to failure."

"Laughter in the Rain" by Neil Sedaka

Neil Sedaka recorded a string of hits in the 1950s and early 1960s, including "Calendar Girl" and "Breaking Up Is Hard to Do." Sedaka's chart success ended as the British Invasion swept America in 1964.

Sedaka launched a comeback in the early 1970s with albums recorded in the UK. While popular in Britain, they failed to catch on in the US.

Enter Elton John, who signed Sedaka to his US label, Rocket Records. He released a compilation album with songs from the British discs, including the single "Laughter in the Rain."

Sedaka wrote "Laughter in the Rain" with lyricist Phil Cody, who described the process in Songfacts.

"Neil had a house in Forestburgh, New York, which is up in the Catskills," said Cody. "We were going to go up there and spend a few days in the summertime and just woodshed.

"The thing is that I'd met a new love and I didn't want to go up there. And when I got there, I was kind of hostile to the whole process. I've never said anything to Neil about this, but as I think about it, I wanted to just get the songs written and get back to the city and my new girlfriend.

"So we got together on a morning, and Neil sat down and played me the changes and the melody to 'Laughter in the Rain.' I just sat there with a blank stare on my face. I had nothing. I had totally nothing.

"I excused myself, and I went out and took a walk. We were up in the country, so I just took a walk and I sat down in a field near a golf course, smoked a joint, and watched some deer frolicking. I spent about an hour and a half, two hours out in the sun, just kind of nodding off under a tree.

"I got myself up a couple of hours later and walked my way back, and Neil was there. I sat down, picked up a yellow pad of paper, and in five minutes I had most of the song done."

When Sedaka heard a version of "Laughter in the Rain" by Lea Roberts on the radio, he called John. Sedaka's version was rush-released in five days and shot to No. 1 in 1975.

"Lay a Little Lovin' on Me" by Robin McNamara

Robin McNamara was a performer in a touring company of Hair when he auditioned for producer Jeff Barry, who signed him to Steed Records. Barry, McNamara, and childhood friend Jim Cretecos wrote "Lay a Little Lovin' on Me," a No. 11 hit in 1970. McNamara told Classic Bands how the bubblegum hit was written.

"When I went down to New York with my ex-wife and son, we were staying with her relations," said McNamara.

"I auditioned and got with Mark Allen. He introduced me to Jeff, and at the time, I could play a few chords on the guitar and the keyboard, but I wasn't that accomplished.

"One of the kids that was in my band back in Boston before I left, his name was Jimmy Cretecos. He played rhythm guitar, but him and I always got together. We would try to write songs together, and we were good friends. We had a good collaboration.

"He was going to Emerson College in Boston. I called him and said, 'Jimmy, I just got a manager and they want to hear some original songs.' I said, 'You've got to quit school and come down. You've got to write with me.'

"Anyway, he quit school, got on his motorcycle, came down, and we started writing together. Him and I started writing together, and then we'd bring material to Jeff to listen to. One of the songs was 'Lay a Little Lovin' on Me.'"

McNamara explained that the song's gospel flavor was intentional.

"I love gospel music and Jeff Barry, if you know anything about his productions and recordings, they all have big hooks. We hired a bunch of girls for the background. I tried to get a little gospel feel into it."

Once the song became a hit, McNamara needed a backing band for concerts.

"Paramount Records, which was the parent company of Steed Records, sent me on promotional tours around the country. I'd go to major markets and minor markets and do local radio and local TV interviews. I would go and perform in certain cities.

"I'd sent my material ahead of time. There'd be a local band that would learn my songs, and I would perform with them. But not all the time."

"Lay Down (Candles in the Rain)" by Melanie with the Edwin Hawkins Singers

Melanie Safka, whose stage name was Melanie, was inspired to write "Lay Down (Candles in the Rain)" during her performance at the 1969 Woodstock Festival. "It started to rain and I actually believed everybody was going to get up and go home," Melanie recalled in Classic Bands.

"Somewhere in my dreams, my hopes, I thought I was going to be saved from having to go do this. I was in total terror. The announcer made some inspirational message about the Hog Farm and passing out candles, and everybody should light a candle.

"Anyway, I was introduced. I went on next. During my set, I got to watch the hillside light up with candles, giving me the inspiration for 'Candles in the Rain.' I wrote it as I was leaving Woodstock."

Melanie recorded "Candle in the Rain" with the Edwin Hawkins Singers, who had recently charted with "Oh Happy Day." When Melanie and her producer and husband, Peter Schekeryk, approached Hawkins, he was reluctant to have his group perform the song.

"When Peter and I talked to Edwin Hawkins, he asked if the Lord was mentioned in my song," Melanie told Vinyl Stories.

"I said, 'Well, not by name, but he's in there.' I wasn't into structured religion. I had given up on all of that. But I had to convince him to do it, because he only did church music. I had to convince him that it was a spiritual song. So he said, 'Let me hear the song and we'll see.'

"Peter and I went out to Oakland, California, where the Edwin Hawkins Singers were rehearsing in a school gymnasium," said Melanie. "I was really shy. It was really hard for me to get up in front of 40 amazing singers and sing my song.

"I was this little white girl, singing and sweating, but after the second chorus, the choir was singing with me, and Edwin Hawkins was really outnumbered. We all marched up to the studio and recorded it in one take.

"It went on for eight minutes, and I still remember Peter doing that universal hand signal for 'One more time,' and we kept going and going, and everybody was getting high off of this song. It was powerful. You live for moments like this."

Buddah Records released a 3:49 version of "Lay Down (Candles in the Rain)" in 1970. It became Melanie's breakthrough hit, reaching No. 6.

"Lead Me On" by Maxine Nightingale

"Lead Me On" was a No. 5 hit in 1979 for Maxine Nightingale, who first gained notice with 1975's "Right Back Where We Started From." "Lead Me On" was written by Allee Willis and David Laskey. Willis explained the song's inspiration in Sonfacts.

"I really was in one of those relationships," said Willis. "It wasn't a bad relationship, but it was one that obviously wasn't gonna work. It was someone that couldn't commit. And I really was a wreck.

"David Lasley was one of the first people I ever collaborated with, and there was a song out at that time that the Bee Gees had written and produced. It was by an artist named Samantha Sang, 'Emotion.'

"So we wanted to write a song that was in kind of that tempo that had that feel, and I don't remember if it was David or me that just said, 'Lead me on.' You know, tease me all night long. I don't care, I want to be in this relationship, you can give me shit, I'm staying here. It was a very mentally unhealthy state to be in.

"That song was written very, very fast, written in under an hour. But I think it was because it was extremely autobiographical."

"Little Willy" by the Sweet

The Sweet's "Little Willy" was written by Nicky Chinn and Mike Chapman, who had a string of bubblegum and glam rock hits in the UK. Chapman exerted tight control over the bands in his stable.

"We were a pretty heavy band when we started and then, unfortunately, one had to pay the rent," bassist Steve Priest told the Phoenix New Times. "That's when Chinn and Chapman came along."

Chinn recalled in AllMusic that the band members hated the song. "Michael and I were definitely autocratic with our bands, and I became aware of that when we were told by the Sweet that 'Little Willy' was a piece of rubbish and had no right to be released.

"It wasn't exactly a symphony, of course, but it was a hit, and we told them it was going to be released, whatever they thought of it."

Chinn and Chapman delivered another hit for the Sweet with 'The Ballroom Blitz,' but as the band began to write songs with a harder edge, they left the songwriting duo. "As soon as we wrote 'Fox on the Run,' Chinn and Chapman were over," said Priest.

"Little Willy," released in 1972, remains the Sweet's biggest hit. The tune reached No. 3 when it was rereleased in 1973. Priest said the band was plagued by bad management.

"They didn't want us to come and tour with 'Little Willy' because it would've given the wrong idea of what the band was all about," said Priest in 2018.

"'Little Willy' still goes down well onstage. I never thought I'd play it again, but I am. We're playing old stuff, doing it better than we did, and spreading the word. We still do 'Blitz' and things because people expect. The idea is not to annoy an audience."

"Lonely Boy" by Andrew Gold

Singer-songwriter Andrew Gold was a multi-instrumentalist and arranger for Linda Ronstadt's 1974 album Heart Like a Wheel and her next two albums before embarking on a solo career. Gold's "Lonely Boy" was his first hit, reaching No. 7 in 1977.

Gold told Classic Bands that "Lonely Boy" was written in about four hours.

"It was gonna be a real long song, because back then that's what people were doing a lot," recalled Gold. "They would cut it down for radio. But I got bored after the third verse.

"Originally, it was not gonna be me at all. But then I thought, just leave it like this. And then we went out and rehearsed the song, played it on the road during my show as a song we hadn't recorded yet. We played it for about two months and really knew it at the end."

Gold recorded "Lonely Boy" with producer Peter Asher and Ronstadt on backing vocals.

"I went into the studio and recorded it live. All of it is live. The song originally had a real plaintive kind of soft section in the middle. And everybody said to hell with that, let's pump it up! And we played it out, and it was much better.

"So when we recorded it, I felt very confident about what we were doing. And we added some strings, and I put the vocal on and that was it."

"Long Tall Glasses (I Can Dance)" by Leo Sayer

"Long Tall Glasses (I Can Dance)" gave Leo Sayer a No. 9 hit in 1975. The song was written by Sayer and David Courtney, who collaborated on Sayer's Just a Boy album.

"It was based on my reaction to success in America," Sayer explained in Rock Cellar.

"I was blown over to be in the States, the place of all my favorite singers like Bobby 'Blue' Bland and B.B. King. They're all telling me I could sing, and I'm going, 'No, I *can't*. Those guys can sing, I can't sing.'

"But they all persuaded me, you can sing, you can sing. So I thought, OK, I'll give in, I can sing, I accept it.

"And in the song, the guy, like Charlie Chaplin in The Gold Rush, goes into the bar and he can't dance, but he's got to get the girl and he's got to impress her. So he pretends, even in his tramp's costume, and he persuades them that he *can* dance."

"Lotta Love" by Nicolette Larson

Nicolette Larson sang on Neil Young's 1977 album American Stars 'n Bars. Both Linda Ronstadt and Emmylou Harris suggested Larson for the gig.

"When he did American Stars 'n Bars, his initial concept was to get two unknown singers and do the album with them, but he tried that and it didn't work at all," Larson recalled in Georgia Straight.

"And then he decided to take the other route and get Emmylou and Linda, but Emmylou wasn't available to do it, so she and Linda recommended me. Neil kind of functions on cosmic operations, you know, and that was cosmic enough for him. If everyone had recommended me, then I was supposed to work with him.

"So Linda and I went up to his ranch and sang backups on that album, and then when he did Comes a Time, he called me again to come and sing on it."

Young wrote and recorded "Lotta Love" in 1976, but he did not release it until 1978's Comes a Time. "He recorded it first," said Larson, "and I heard it and said, 'Gee, that's great. How come you don't put that song out?' And he goes, 'Oh, do you want it? It's yours.'

"That was what he said with every song of his that I admired. It was kind of like, 'Don't ask me why I don't put this out. You want to put it out, you put it out.'

Larson recorded "Lotta Love" for her 1978 debut album, Nicolette. Producer Ted Templeman told Rolling Stone that as the end of the sessions neared, he was having trouble coming up with an arrangement for the song—until he heard Ace's "How Long" on the drive to the studio.

"I got in the studio and I said, 'Don't talk, everybody!' and I played the chords," said Templeman. He added a saxophone line and a disco bass run to the arrangement. "I stole that whole chord change," said Templeman, "to put an intro."

Larson had completed the album when Young had a change of heart about his original. "I recorded it, and got it all ready to put out, then at the very last minute he changed his mind on Comes a Time and put it on that," said Larson.

"So we both released it the very same day, actually. I changed it around quite a lot from Neil's version. His is a lot different with all the 'la la la la's' at the beginning."

"Lotta Love" was Larson's biggest hit, reaching No. 8 in 1979. "It was a very positive song and people don't want to hear how bad the world is all the time," Larson told the Free Lance-Star. "It had a nice sound rhythm and groove. And a great visual video."

"Love Grows (Where My Rosemary Goes)" by Edison Lighthouse

Tony Macaulay and co-writer Barry Mason struck gold in 1970 with "Love Grows." Macaulay recorded the song with prolific bubblegum vocalist Tony Burrows, backed by session musicians.

"I had done some recording for the musical director on that particular record, a guy called Lou Warburton," Burrows told Pop Entertainment.

"I was doing backing vocals, in actual fact, for Tony Macaulay, who was recording a lot of his titles. I happened to have a tape of a track, which Lou wanted to hear. I asked everybody, 'Would you mind if I play the track in the studio for Lou?'

"They said, no, go ahead, which I did, and he listened, and after he did, he came up and asked if I would like to sing lead on 'Love Grows.'"

When "Love Grows" reached No. 5 in 1970, a touring band had to be formed. Macaulay chose the Greenfield Hammer. Burrows, however, was tired of touring and is not seen in the song's videos.

"That was because I still refused to tour while the groups all continued to record and do television," Burrows explained in Rebeat.

"I wasn't around. Once the song became a hit, they wanted to do an album and book these groups for concerts, but I wasn't going to do that. So what they'd do is find someone to lip sync the song and film it so the listeners would recognize that person as the lead singer when they were on tour."

"Lovin' You" by Minnie Riperton

"Lovin' You" was written by Minnie Riperton and her husband, Richard Rudolph. When Riperton signed with Epic Records, the label asked whom she would like to produce her 1974 album, Perfect Angel, which included the song. Riperton's response: Stevie Wonder.

Wonder, who was a fan of Riperton's work, agreed to co-produce the album with Rudolph. Because Wonder was under contract to Motown Records, he used the pseudonym "El Toro Negro," Spanish for "The Black Bull."

Rudolph explained in OkayPlayer how "Lovin' You" was written at their home in Gainesville, FL.

"Minnie was in the kitchen singing, and I was playing the guitar in the other room, and suddenly, she started singing something, and I went, 'What?' That stuck, and I knew that we had it.

"We tried to record 'Lovin' You' three or four different ways. One day, Stevie said, 'Let's listen to the original demo,' which we had recorded in Gainesville with me on guitar and Minnie singing. He said, 'Let's do it that way.'

"Stevie said, 'Just put the guitar down the way you played it. The way you wrote it.' I went into the studio with a click track and with these two fools sitting in the studio trying to make me laugh over the headphones, while I was trying to record the track. Stevie and Minnie were in there saying the most terrible things into my headphones while I'm trying to play, and they thought it was hysterical.

"We finally got it down, and then blessedly and blissfully, Stevie came in and played the two gorgeous Fender Rhodes parts over the guitar. It's just me and him on the track. We listened to it, and we thought it was so beautiful.

"Minnie said, 'Something's still missing.' We didn't think we should add bass or drums or anything. It was a beautiful, separate reality.

"We went back and listened to the demo again from our place in Gainesville. The window had been open, and there was a bird singing outside. Stevie said, 'Get the bird.'

"We went out to the UCLA Botanical Garden with his Nagra tape recorder, and Minnie would sit there and try to sing these really high bird calls and get birds to sing."

When the track was completed, Epic refused to release "Lovin' You" as a single despite the reaction the song received in concert.

"We came back and said to the label, 'You've got to put this out,'" said Rudolph. "They responded, 'You can't do it. She's a black singer and she's got no bass and no drums.' All the experts told us, but we just kept arguing and trying.

"Then, we put it out, and you know what happened. It was like magic."

"Lovin' You" topped the Billboard chart in 1975. It was the biggest hit of Riperton's career, shortened by her death at 31 from cancer in 1979.

"Magnet and Steel" by Walter Egan

Singer-songwriter Walter Egan recorded "Magnet and Steel" for his 1978 second album, Not Shy. Stevie Nicks and Lindsey Buckingham of Fleetwood Mac performed background vocals. Egan told Rock Cellar that Nicks was his inspiration for the song.

"My intention in writing 'Magnet' was to express my infatuation for Stevie Nicks," Egan told Rock Cellar. "I believe that the record was made that much more special when she sang on it with me."

Nicks and Buckingham also assisted on Egan's 1977 debut album, Fundamental Roll. Egan said in Classic Bands that "Magnet and Steel" was born out of one of the album's recording sessions.

"The chrysalis of that song happened one night when Stevie was singing the background vocals on my first song called 'Tunnel of Love,' where she does her wild Banshee wail on the background of it. For whatever reason, it stirred some things in me that night.

"I was living out in Pomona at the time, and on my way home, I got on the 101 Freeway, and this car got in front of me. It was just one of those completely customized Continentals with the lights under it and the diamond window. I couldn't help but notice the license plate said Not Shy and for whatever reason, I took that as a message and I ran with it.

"In the 30 to 40-minute drive to Pomona, I had put the rest of the song together. So ultimately it took me about half an hour once I sat down with a pen to write out those lyrics."

"Magnet and Steel" was Egan's first and only hit, reaching No. 8 in 1978.

"No artist sets out to be a one-hit wonder, and the phrase itself implies a flash in the pan, someone who just got lucky through situation and circumstance," said Egan.

"Yes, I am a one-hit wonder. I, of course, feel it's a wonder that I only had one hit. By the way, Jimi Hendrix is also a one-hit wonder. That said, I am not defined by that status."

"Makin' It" by David Naughton

Actor David Naughton is best known for his starring role in the 1981 film An American Werewolf in London. Naughton first became widely known for his singing and dancing in Dr Pepper TV commercials. The ads, which ran from 1977 to 1981, led to his being cast by ABC in a 1979 TV show.

"I was on a series called Makin' It, which was really loosely based on Saturday Night Fever, which was of course a big hit and phenomenon," Naughton told Cryptic Rock.

"This series was an ABC disco show, so I had an opportunity to go knock down the door to go meet the people who were putting the music together. I told them, 'I sing, I have done all these Dr Pepper jingles, I would certainly like the chance to record the title song.'"

"Makin' It" was written by Dino Fekaris and Freddie Perren. Naughton recorded the theme, his only musical release, which was released in 1979.

"I had to sort of win that role and got a chance to sing the song that was released on RSO Records, with Robert Stigwood, who had the Bee Gees. The song went to number 5 in the Top 40.

"I had no idea it was going to be a successful song. You just never know, you go in sometimes with an open mind, give your all, and lo and behold, things work out."

"Mandy" by Barry Manilow

Originally titled "Brandy," Barry Manilow's 1974 No. 1 smash "Mandy" was written by British songwriters Scott English and Richard Kerr. English had a No. 12 hit in the UK with his version.

Manilow was introduced to the song by Clive Davis, head of Arista Records. "I fought it because I was the songwriter," Manilow told the Television Academy.

"I didn't want somebody else's song. But I listened to it — it was 'Brandy,' a rock and roll song. I thought, what am I going to do with this?"

Manilow went into the studio with producer Ron Dante and dutifully recorded a version that stuck to English's original.

"I sang it as-is, and we invited Clive down," said Manilow. "He said, 'What's that?' I said, 'That's what you just gave me.' He said, 'That's terrible.' I said, 'I know.'

"But during the afternoon, in order to learn 'Brandy,' I had slowed it down and — just because I wanted to — I'd changed the chords around and put in a key change. But then I forgot about it and played Clive the rock and roll song. But now I went to the piano and played him the ballad version of 'Brandy' with my key and chord changes.

"He said, 'Do that. And we can't use Brandy. Sing Mandy,'" a reference to the Looking Glass hit "Brandy (You're a Fine Girl)."

"So we changed the name. I played the slow version, we put a small band behind it, and added 'Mandy' to that second album. And my life changed."

"I, of course, didn't want to like it," English recalled in the liner notes of Manilow's The Complete Collection . . . And Then Some.

"You know what it is, ego and all that, but it sounded very beautiful," said English. "This record went on to shake the rafters of the world—just as I knew it would when we were writing it way back when."

"Me and You and a Dog Named Boo" by Lobo

Lobo is the pseudonym of singer-songwriter Kent LaVoie. Lobo's biggest hit was "Me and You and a Dog Named Boo," which reached No. 5 in 1971. LaVoie told Classic Bands that when his producer, Phil Gernhard, brought him to a meeting in New York, he was inspired to write the tune.

"He took me up to the publisher of Famous Music and a guy named Billy Meshel, chief song plugger at the time. Phil sat me down with Billy. We were talking about music in general. This was in 1969.

"He said, 'What's goin' on right now, it's kids going out in the world and doing things, blah, blah, blah.'"

The meeting gave LaVoie a direction to take with his next song. LaVoie explained what happened next on MyBestYears.com.

"I was working on several songs, including a tune about traveling around the country with this girl, and I was trying to rhyme 'you and me.' Now 'me and you' would have been easier, but I was trying to do it with proper grammar.

"I couldn't find anything to rhyme that fit what I wanted to say in the song. Finally, after I got back home to Florida, I decided to turn the phrase around to 'me and you.'

"I was thinking about it, sitting in a room that had a big sliding glass door overlooking the backyard. My big German Shepherd dog, Boo, came running around the corner and looked in at me. I said, 'Well, now, that's kinda freaky. How about putting "a dog named Boo" into the song?'

"That's literally how it came about. All of a sudden, the song really started coming together. I hadn't been to any of the places mentioned in the song except Georgia, but I just kept putting in places that sounded far away, like Minneapolis and LA."

"Me and You and a Dog Named Boo" was released on Lobo's 1971 debut album, Introducing Lobo.

"It was studio musicians," said LaVoie. "I never had a band. It was always just me.

"The first album, because the record hit so fast, we had to hurry and get this album done. I don't know why they didn't do a photo session. They just used a stock picture they found with a guy and a dog sitting around a campfire.

"It's got nothing to do with me. I was always behind this stuff and nobody ever knew, until years later, that it was just one person."

"Midnight at the Oasis" by Maria Muldaur

Maria Muldaur was not a solo performer when she broke up with her husband, Geoff Muldaur, in 1972. The Muldaurs had performed with the Jim Kweskin Jug Band. As a young, single mother, she had to support herself and her daughter.

Everything changed when Mo Ostin, president of Warner Bros. Records, offered Muldaur the chance to record a solo album.

"I had been working a little bit with a young guitar player named David Nichtern, who played great guitar and wrote really lovely, contemporary songs," Muldaur told Pennyblackmusic.

"When we started the recording, I found myself in the studio with all the top guns of the recording world at that time. Dr. John, Ry Cooder, David Lyndley, Jim Keltner, all the greats. I was planning to record one of David's songs, a lovely ballad called 'I Never Did Sing You a Love Song.'"

Nichtern drove to Los Angeles and attended the sessions, hoping to play rhythm guitar on the track.

The producer Lenny Waronker came in," said Muldaur, "and he says, 'I've been listening to the rough tracks at home and I think that we're in pretty good shape. We've got some nice ballads, and we have some great uptempo songs. I think if we could just find one medium-tempo song to round out the album, I think we'd be in great shape.'

"I thought to myself, David has a song. It's kind of a funny little song, but it's the right tempo. So I said, 'David, why don't you play "Midnight at the Oasis" for him?' I wasn't wild about the song, but it did fulfill the qualifications of being medium-tempo. David whipped out his guitar and started to play it, and I sang it.

"The producer cocks his head to the side, and I could tell he wasn't wild about it either, but he says, 'That's cute, do you want to do that? Let's do that." I did this strictly as a gesture of gratitude to David for being so supportive."

"Midnight at the Oasis" was released on Muldaur's 1973 debut album, Maria Muldaur.

"After a couple of months of it just climbing the charts on its own," said Muldaur. "DJs just started playing cuts, and all of a sudden there was a huge request for 'Midnight at the Oasis.'"

The tune became a No. 6 hit in mid-1974.

"I had never thought they'd make it a single," explained Muldaur. "It became a gold record, eventually platinum. It was nominated for a Grammy in several categories. It put me on the map, not just in this country, but around the world.

"So that's the story of 'Midnight at the Oasis' and I'm stickin' to it!"

"Midnight Blue" by Melissa Manchester

"Midnight Blue" was Melissa Manchester's first Top 10 hit, reaching No. 6 in 1975. Manchester wrote "Midnight Blue" with lyricist Carole Bayer Sager. "It's very conversational because all of our songs came out of conversations," Manchester told Songfacts.

"At the time, we were young married women trying to navigate some stormy waters in our young marriages, trying to find language to help clarify our communication with our young husbands, and the way we would find clarity is through our songs."

Manchester explained their songwriting process in HuffPost. "Carole would show up with lyrics and then we would talk about it and work on lyrics and musical progressions," said Manchester.

"It's partially like having an alternative voice, and everything comes out in a gush, probably because the chemicals in the brain are on overload from being able to experience this new form of communication. As you get deeper into the process of writing, what takes over is the craft of writing. You start to polish things and be more mindful of rhymes or rhythms.

"'Midnight Blue' is so touching for me," Manchester explained. "First of all, it was my first hit, and second, and most importantly, there's a certain suggestion of world weariness in the song. We wrote it as such young women, and to be singing the song decades later and to have grown into that real-world weariness is interesting and touching. It's like those young women who wrote that such a long time ago knew about what was to come."

"Moonlight Feels Right" by Starbuck

"Moonlight Feels Right" is the debut single by Starbuck. Written by singer and keyboardist Bruce Blackman, it featured a prominent marimba solo by co-founder Bo Wagner. As Blackman told Goldmine, it took determination to achieve success.

"After we recorded our music," said Blackman, "it was turned down by every major label in America for two reasons. They would say, 'It's not southern rock and it's not disco.'

"We didn't want to do that because that was what everybody else was doing, plus the instrumentation was built around my songs, using my Minimoog and Bo's skills with marimba, vibes, tympani, and a ton of instruments.

"Private Stock was the last label we went to, and they liked 'Moonlight Feels Right' but wanted us to cut the marimba solo out, saying it was too long. I don't know how I had the guts to refuse to do that, but I did.

"The record came out in September of 1975. The team at Private Stock sent it out to a couple dozen of the top radio stations, and nothing happened, so Bo and I bought 500 of our own records from the label; they wouldn't give them to us.

"Bo headed east, and I headed west. We started pulling into towns, looking for radio towers. If we thought the station's format fit our music, we would go in and leave a record."

WERC in Birmingham, AL, showed interest but said that it sounded like a spring song and they would play it then. The station kept its promise and became the first station to play the tune. It helped "Moonlight Feels Right" reach No. 3 in 1976.

"Motorcycle Mama" by Sailcat

The breezy 1972 hit "Motorcycle Mama" was recorded by Sailcat, a Southern pop rock group that was essentially John Wyker and Court Pickett, two veterans of the Muscle Shoals music scene. The one-hit wonder band was hastily assembled after "Motorcycle Mama" became a No. 12 hit.

"Motorcycle Mama" is the title track of a concept album recorded with studio musicians that capitalized on the popularity of biker films. "I called it a rock opera," Wyker explained in the album's liner notes.

"The storyline behind Motorcycle Mama is really simple to understand. It's about a no-good riding motorcycle tramp that is really a latent romantic, and has dreams of settling down and having a family."

But the song was almost roadkill before it was even released. The night it was recorded, Wyker said, "We get a motel, come back, listened to what we did, and I said, 'Oh, man, this is the worst thing I ever heard in my life.' And I took the tape and literally threw it in the garbage can."

Fortunately, Elektra Records heard a copy and signed Wyker and Pickett. When "Motorcycle Mama" rose on the charts, the two had to put together a touring band and come up with a name.

"The name came from a Jonathan Winters record," said Wyker, "where a sailcat is a cat that's been run over so many times on the highway that you can scoop him up and throw him like a Frisbee."

Despite its success, Wyker remained dismissive of Elektra and the tune.

"I cussed the label out from the stage of Carnegie Hall. Somebody said 'Motorcycle Mama!' I said, 'You know, I hate that song. It's just so wussy. I had thrown it in a garbage can and somebody fished it out and these double-domed eggheads from LA thought it could be a hit, and they made it a hit, and I'm ashamed of it."

"My Baby Loves Lovin'" by White Plains

Before he became the anonymous voice of bands like Edison Lighthouse, who released "Love Grows (Where My Rosemary Goes}," and the Brotherhood of Man, who hit with "United We Stand," Tony Burrows was a member of the Flower Pot Men, a British pop band. Burrows explained in Rebeat how that led to his recording "My Baby Loves Lovin'" as the band White Plains.

"What actually happened was the Flower Pot Men did that song, but then I quit because I didn't want to tour anymore. I got a call that the record company wanted to release some of our unreleased tracks, and I said that that was fine.

"The song was released as being by White Plains, and it was a hit, so the group got back together again. But not me; I'd had enough of touring.

"I sang on the first couple of records, but that was it. I just wasn't going to do it. I was just going to concentrate on studio work."

Written by Roger Cook and Roger Greenaway, "My Baby Loves Lovin'" reached No. 13 on the Billboard chart in 1970.

"My Maria" by B.W. Stevenson

Singer-songwriter Daniel Moore wrote "Shambala," a near-simultaneous release in 1973 by country pop singer B.W.

Stevenson and Three Dog Night. Stevenson's version never gained much traction, reaching No. 66. Three Dog Night had a No. 3 hit with the tune about a mythical kingdom.

Stevenson's producer David Kirshenbaum hoped Moore had another song for his artist because, Moore recalled in Songfacts, "B.W.'s version died on the vine.

"That's when David Kirshenbaum called me and asked if I had any other songs in the same groove as 'Shambala.' I told him I had an unfinished song called 'My Maria' that was the same basic feel.

"He asked if I would consider letting B.W. help finish the song. I told him I'd be open to trying. We met at the big RCA Studio in Hollywood.

"I made a cassette recording of what I had: the guitar part, the opening line of lyrics, and the melody, plus the words and melody of the chorus. B.W. went in a room by himself and wrote the rest of the lyrics in about 15 minutes. I had been working on that music for at least two years.

"We made a cassette of B.W. singing the new lyrics and me playing the guitar part. We called an arranger, who got there in about 20 minutes. Two days later, with top L.A. musicians, we cut 'My Maria.'"

Stevenson's "My Maria" became a No. 9 hit in 1973.

"I think that radio felt sorry for B.W. because Three Dog had run over him with 'Shambala.' So radio played the heck out of 'My Maria.' One month after 'My Maria' was written, it was a hit."

"Nice to Be with You" by Gallery

Gallery was a soft rock band formed in Detroit by singer-songwriter Jim Gold. Gold was discovered by guitarist

Dennis Coffey and arranger Mike Theodore. Gallery's biggest hit was "Nice to Be with You," which reached No. 4 in 1972.

Gold told Classic Bands that the catchy tune "came to me during the day when I was working. My mind was always kind of wandering 'cause my job was really boring. By the time I got home, it was already formulated in my head. I ran in the door, picked up my acoustic guitar, wrote it down, and that was it. I'd say 15 minutes, 20 minutes."

Coffey and Theodore signed Gold to Sussex Records, and Gallery was formed with Gold's childhood friend Bill Nova and studio musicians.

"When I first played it for them guys, they thought well, yeah, it's OK," recalled Gold.

"They kind of brushed over it. When we actually got in to record it and when it was coming together and Mike put the bells and different things on it, we really didn't know what the Gallery sound was going to be. We were kind of forced into having a group name because that's what was happening at the time.

"I came up with the name. We figured it was generic enough it could be anything. When they said, 'What do you want this to sound like?' and here we are in the suburbs of Detroit, and the sounds around here are Motown, Bob Seger. Industrial Rock and R&B.

"I said, 'No, nothing like that. You're going to think I'm crazy, but I would like to hear a steel guitar on here.' They said, 'A what?' And I said, 'A steel guitar.'

"I'm glad Mike and Dennis went along with it. Normally, they would say, 'We've done some records and that's not gonna fly. You'll have to try something else.' But they gave me the benefit of the doubt because what I was writing was a combination of pop songs, love ballads, and story songs, which they really liked."

Gold described in Goldmine hearing "Nice to Be with You" on the radio for the first time.

"I was driving to work at this crap job at a steel company where I was working during the day, after playing music at nighttime," said Gold.

"I was half asleep. I turned on CKLW, and I started singing the song and humming it, and I didn't even realize it at first that it was me. When I did, I pulled off to the side of the road and said, 'Oh my God!'

"I called my wife on the phone and said, 'You've got to wake the kids up. You are not going to believe this. CKLW is playing 'Nice to Be with You.' She said, 'What? I didn't know it was released.' I said, 'I didn't know either.'"

"Nobody Does It Better" by Carly Simon

"Nobody Does It Better" by Carly Simon was the theme of the 1977 James Bond film The Spy Who Loved Me. Marvin Hamlisch was working with lyricist Carole Bayer Sager when he confided that he was hired to write the theme for the film. Bayer Sager immediately suggested the title "Nobody Does It Better."

"I don't know how I came up with it," she wrote in her memoir, They're Playing Our Song. "I just thought about James Bond, and that's what popped out of my mouth.

"Marvin instantly loved it and within seconds we'd both forgotten the song we'd gotten together to write and he was playing the melody of the chorus."

"Nobody Does It Better" was one of Carly Simon's biggest hits, reaching No. 2 in 1977. The song received Academy

Award and Golden Globe Award nominations for Best Original Song in 1978.

"I think 'Nobody Does It Better' was the perfect song and I was the perfect artist for it at the time," Simon told Billboard.

"When I first auditioned the song, it was just before Christmas, and I was expecting my tax lawyer to come over for some reason to my apartment. I was very pregnant with my son Ben.

"I had a one o'clock appointment with my tax lawyer, but I had somehow made an appointment that conflicted with the tax appointment guy. So the doorbell rang at one o'clock, and this man came in. He was obviously the tax lawyer. He had horn-rimmed glasses and a work suit.

"I said, 'Why don't you wait in the living room?' He waited in the living room, and I asked him if he'd like a cup of tea, and he said, 'Yes, I would very much.'"

While Simon was in the kitchen, the melody of "Nobody Does It Better" came from the piano in the living room.

"It was Marvin Hamlisch looking like a tax lawyer! He played the song for me, and it was a natural right away. It just fit my voice. It was quite wonderful."

The song was produced by Richard Perry. Careful listeners will hear Simon say, "James, you're the best" at the end of the song during the fade-out.

"As I recorded my vocal, I imagined how the movie would start," Simon said in the Wall Street Journal.

"Bond films always had plenty of action before the theme song came on. I also felt Carole's female perspective in the lyrics. They fit me perfectly. Adding 'James, you're the best' was the perfect homage."

"No No Song" by Ringo Starr

Hoyt Axton's use of drugs and alcohol inspired his "No No Song," written with bassist David Jackson. Axton told the Oklahoman that he wrote the song one morning and didn't know what hotel—or city—he was in. Axton said he feared that he was dead.

"I was afraid if I looked around, I'd see the devil sittin' in the chair across the room, sayin' 'I got'cha, boy. You finally overdid it,'" said Axton. "That was the day before I wrote the 'No No Song.'

"It wasn't really that much of a moral issue. It was just my body started sayin', 'Now wait a minute.'

"A good analogy would be that your life is a camera and your mind is the lens. If you've got something foggin' up the lens, man, you're not gonna get a clear picture, a clear set of memories, or a clear life.

"I just got tired of bein' drunk and crazed."

"No No Song" was a No. 3 hit for Ringo Starr in 1975. "Love the song," Starr told Paste. "Love what it was doing. It was such a good song for me. Real, but comedy. Good lyric, good attitude. Makes no sense. Good song for me."

The songwriter joined Starr in the studio, which the drummer called a "magical experience with Hoyt Axton." Starr was not sober when he recorded the anti-drug, anti-alcohol tune.

"We were doing 'No No Song' with the biggest spliff and a large bottle of Jack Daniel's," Starr admitted in Time. It would not be until 1988 that Starr entered rehab.

"I have great memories of when we recorded that, because the last thing any of us were doing was saying 'no' in those days," Starr told the Associated Press. "Things have changed, of course."

"On and On" by Stephen Bishop

Singer-songwriter Stephen Bishop followed his 1977 hit "Save It for a Rainy Day" later that year with "On and On," which reached No. 11. Bishop told American Songwriter that he was inspired by his landlady's garden.

"My landlady back then used to put lots of flowers in her garden from all over the world," said Bishop. "She was a big flower lady.

"So she would tell me where all these flowers were from. And back then, I hadn't traveled anywhere. So I was really fascinated by that.

"And then I was walking down the street to the corner grocery store, and I just got the idea for the title. I just wrote it down in my little message book. When I went back to my apartment, I came up with this chord that I just loved. Then I just kept playing it over and over, and I finally did something with it, and made 'On and On.'"

"On and On" opens with the couplet "Down in Jamaica they got lots of pretty women / Steal your money then they break your heart." The lyrics earned Bishop blowback at a Hollywood party he attended with Jamaican reggae star Bob Marley's wife, Rita.

"She started screaming at me," Bishop said in the Houston Press.

"'You do *not* know about Jamaican women! They do *not* steal your money!' I was scared to death because she was really livid! I was just, uh, 'poetic license?' I spent the rest of the party hiding out in the kitchen."

"One Less Bell to Answer" by the Fifth Dimension

"One Less Bell to Answer" was written by Hal David and Burt Bacharach. The songwriting giants disagreed on its origin. Bacharach said in Songwriters on Songwriting that his then-girlfriend, actress Angie Dickinson, inspired the title.

"That was kind of a freak that it happened," said Bacharach. "The title was born from working on 'What's New Pussycat,' and Angie Dickinson was living with me in London.

"A doorbell rang, and I think she made the comment, 'One less bell to answer, when I get out of here.' It was pretty intense, and it bothered her. We weren't married yet, but we were living together.

"I think Hal heard her say, 'One less bell to answer.' He thought, That's a good song title, and we wrote it."

"Burt and I were in London working on a project, and I was invited to a dinner party," David recalled in the liner notes of The Look of Love box set.

"The hostess said to me, 'When you arrive, don't ring the bell, just come in. It'll make one less bell for me to answer.' I was wise enough to know it was a good title!"

Keely Smith was the first to record 'One Less Bell to Answer" in 1967. Marilyn McCoo of the Fifth Dimension told Spotlight Central that the group discovered the song at a "listening session."

"Whenever we'd get ready to record, we would have what we called 'listening sessions,'" McCoo recalled. "Before the sessions, our producer, Bones Howe, would go through a ton of music—he had such an incredible ear, and he could hear songs that really had potential—and he would wade through those songs and bring us what he thought were the best ones for us to listen to.

"And he brought us 'One Less Bell' which, interestingly enough, was a demo that was performed by Dionne Warwick. And Bones played it, and he said, 'I thought, Marilyn, that you could do this.'

"And I said, 'Oh, I love it—you know, I love torch songs! But Dionne Warwick is singing it—why doesn't Dionne Warwick record it?' And Bones said, 'Well, we don't know why she didn't record it, but do you want to sing it or not?' And I said, 'Yes! I want to sing it!'"

With McCoo performing lead vocals, the Fifth Dimension hit No. 2 with "One Less Bell to Answer" in 1970.

"Peace Train" by Cat Stevens

"Peace Train" was a No. 7 hit in 1971 for Cat Stevens, who changed his name to Yusuf Islam when he became a Muslim in 1977.

"I love trains," Stevens explained in Songwriter Universe. "And we were growing up in a time where war was always looking imminent, with the Cold War and everything. And then there was Vietnam, and you'd see these images of destruction and killing.

"I think there was war everywhere. Then there was obviously the movement—the Campaign for Nuclear Disarmament, which is CND, which is where you get that peace sign from. That movement was very strong, and it was growing stronger.

"So I wanted to write about this search for peace, and then I got this idea to link it with a train—the idea about peace with the peace train.

"The other thing is, the peace train is a symbol of mankind traveling together towards the same destination. Because we all have similar goals. Happiness is definitely universal—it's what we all want. So that's where 'Peace Train' comes in."

"Playground in My Mind" by Clint Holmes

"Playground in My Mind" is a nursery rhyme-styled tune written by Paul Vance and Lee Pockriss. It was first recorded by Billy Lawrence in 1971 as "Playground in My Mind (Mama, Je T'aime)" but did not chart.

It was a chance meeting in 1972 that brought the song to Clint Holmes. "I had really just started my career," Holmes told NPR.

"I had gotten out of the Army and started singing locally in Washington, DC. I got a job singing in the Bahamas. We didn't have a dressing room, and we did two or three shows a night.

"So after one of the shows one night, I go into the men's room to wash my face and wait for the elevator to go up to my room, and a guy walks up and he says, 'You sound a little bit like Johnny Mathis, and I produce Johnny Mathis. I wrote this song and that song for Johnny Mathis, and I have a song for you.' I was skeptical, but I said okay."

That man was Paul Vance, who was on vacation in the Bahamas.

"When I finished that job, I went to New York, and he played me that song, and he went 'My name is Michael. I got it a nickel . . .' I didn't like it. I thought it was way too cutesy. I wanted to sing Marvin Gaye or Roberta Flack. That was my self-image.

"But it was an opportunity. So I made the record. I recorded it in 1972. It came out and kind of did nothing. Then someone programmed it as a Christmas record that year.

"It went from nothing in the middle of '72 to a Christmas record at the end of '72 to a big hit by the middle of '73. I was very lucky. It was just a novelty song that just found its place."

Vance's seven-year-old son Philip performed as Michael on the record. "Playground in My Mind" rose to No. 2 in 1973 and was Holmes' only hit.

"Poetry Man" by Phoebe Snow

"Poetry Man' was written by Phoebe Snow for her self-titled 1974 debut album. It became Snow's first hit, reaching No. 5 in 1975. Its lyric, "Home's that place somewhere you go each day / To see your wife," reflected her real-life romance with a married man.

"That was the second song I ever wrote in my whole life; the first one so lame I hardly remember it," Snow recalled in Creative Loafing.

"It was just an exercise for me. I was trying so hard to be this hip and groovy person. I was so stupid.

"The second one, 'Poetry Man,' came about because I was really getting the hang of guitar picking, and I had these open chords, not open tuning, open chords. And I was having a relationship with somebody.

"From the words, you can probably deduce that the guy was married. It was a bad thing to do. But I got a lovely romantic sonnet out of it."

"As it turns out, he was not a particularly great guy either. I turned it into this ode to romance. It's funny looking back on it—I sat there and hunched over the guitar and said, 'I'm gonna finish this.' I was in the throes of young romance. "Twenty or 21. It came right out, a finished product, within an hour or so."

By 1998, Snow had a different take on the song's meaning. "My head was in a particular place when I wrote that song, which condones extramarital relations, which now I do not at all condone," she told the Minneapolis Star Tribune.

"I was a silly kid back then who had no idea what was going on, and I had sex with a married man. How can I stand up there now and sing what purports to be this little romantic ditty about sleeping with somebody else's husband? That makes me crazy.

"I'm glad I'm saying this publicly because I don't like to preach during my shows. I just like to entertain.

"Now I sound like an old fart. But I just think extramarital affairs bring sorrow and bad karma. It's just really a bad idea."

"Reminiscing" by the Little River Band

"Reminiscing" is one of the Little River Band's signature songs. The lead vocalist was Glenn Shorrock, and it was written by the Australian band's rhythm guitarist Graeham Goble, who explained its creation in Guitar Player.

"It was inspired by my love of the '30s, '40s, and '50s musicals, 'cause I was 12 years of age when we got a black-and-white television in Adelaide," said Goble.

"The programs I immediately loved were all the Fred Astaire-Ginger Rogers, Rogers and Hammerstein musicals—all of that American romantic era. A lot of my songwriting, but particularly 'Reminiscing,' was about the life I wished I had, putting myself into those situations I saw in the movies."

Lead guitarist David Briggs played an unfamiliar chord for Goble that set the song in motion.

"I picked up my Martin 000-18 and played that chord. Immediately, I had this melody and lyric, all at the same time, almost like it was a spiritual download that just flowed through me. In about half an hour, the whole thing was finished, and I had this very different song with key changes and quite a lot of jazz chords—quite a sophisticated piece!"

Two recording attempts were unsuccessful, and the song was almost abandoned.

"The keyboard player I wanted for it was Peter Jones, and he was not available," said Goble. "So I was forced to pick another player, and it didn't work. And then we did it with a second player, and that didn't work out, either.

"Then I heard Peter Jones had come back into town. So, under protest from some of the guys, mainly from Glenn Shorrock, they reluctantly agreed to give it a third go. As soon as we sat down with Peter, the whole thing came together."

"Reminiscing" was a No. 3 hit in 1978. In her book Loving John, May Pang wrote that she and John Lennon would often lie in bed and listen to "Reminiscing."

Goble called the tune "our pinnacle song. It's been in a lot of movies and a lot of soundtracks. Sinatra said he thought it was the best '70s song in the world, though he never recorded it. But when John Lennon calls your song one of his favorites, does that really matter?"

"Reunited" by Peaches & Herb

Linda Greene was not the first or last singer to perform as Peaches with Herb Fame. Seven women have accompanied Fame since the duo formed in 1966. Greene, the third Peaches, sang on the disco hit "Shake Your Groove Thing" and "Reunited," a No. 1 pop and R&B smash.

"Reunited" was written by Dino Fekaris and Freddie Perren and was produced by Perren. To avoid the label as a disco act, said Greene, Fame "decided to make our next release something totally different. We went for an R&B ballad, and that was 'Reunited.'"

Greene described in the Indie Post how "Reunited" was selected.

"I sat in the recording room, in the dark listening to three demo songs," said Greene. "I started getting goosebumps.

"Right before the lyrics began on the last of the three songs, I believe I heard God's voice speak to me for the first time. That voice said this song is going to change your life and many others.

"When I came out of that room, I felt like someone who had just left the planet. They asked me if I selected the song. I said yes, we're going to do 'Reunited.'"

"When Peaches first heard 'Reunited,' she started to cry," Perren told Blues & Soul in 1980, "while Herb just stood there shaking his head."

"That was the ultimate song on the album for me," added Greene. "It was overwhelming just to listen to the words of that song. It was not written about myself and Herb as a couple's relationship. Dino Fekaris and Freddie wrote it for the people who could truly relate to it."

"Rhiannon" by Fleetwood Mac

Vocalist Stevie Nicks of Fleetwood Mac wrote "Rhiannon" after reading Triad: A Novel of the Supernatural by Mary Bartlet Leader, a story of witches and ghosts.

"It was just a stupid little paperback that I found somewhere at somebody's house, lying on the couch," Nicks told Classic Rock.

"It was called Triad, and it was all about this girl who becomes possessed by a spirit named Rhiannon. I read the book, but I was so taken with that name that I thought, 'I've got to write something about this.'

"So I sat down at the piano and started this song about a woman that was all involved with these birds and magic."

"Rhiannon" was released in 1976 as a single from Fleetwood Mac's 1975 eponymous album and reached No. 11. Nicks delivered intense performances of "Rhiannon" in concert, and it became her signature song.

"'Rhiannon' is the heavy-duty song to sing every night," she told Crawdaddy. "On stage, it's really a mind tripper. Everybody, including me, is just blitzed by the end of it.

"And I put out so much in that song that I'm nearly down. There's something to that song that touches people. I don't know what it is, but I'm really glad it happened."

"She's not a person that half-cooks anything," Mick Fleetwood told VH1, "so her 'Rhiannon' in those days was like an exorcism."

"Rhinestone Cowboy" by Glen Campbell

"Rhinestone Cowboy" was written and first recorded by Larry Weiss, who released it on his 1974 album Black and

Blue Suite. The song barely dented the charts but received airplay on an easy listening station in Los Angeles.

"I first heard the song on KNX-FM in Los Angeles," Glen Campbell recalled in Billboard. "I called my secretary and said I've got to get a song called 'Rhinestone Cowboy' by somebody. I don't remember who.

"Meanwhile, I stumbled into Al Coury's office at Capitol Records, and he said he had a record he wanted me to hear. And he played me 'Rhinestone Cowboy.'"

"I had heard the phrase 'rhinestone cowboy' somewhere, and it stuck," Weiss told The Guardian in 2013. "When I moved to Nashville 20 years ago, I finally found out that it meant rhinestone-studded country singers of the '50s and '60s. But I gave it my own spin.

"When I was a kid, I loved cowboy movies: Roy Rogers, Gene Autry, and Hopalong Cassidy. To me, the singing cowboys were the rhinestone cowboys."

Campbell scored a No. 1 hit in 1975 with "Rhinestone Cowboy." Co-producer Dennis Lambert told The Guardian he was surprised that Campbell reacted positively to the song.

"Glen doesn't mince words," said Lambert. "He either feels something and jumps right on it, or he doesn't; he thought the song was great.

"We didn't copy Larry's version, but took the essence of it, which was right on the money. Why fix something that isn't broken?

"I did have doubts that a major star would connect with a song about a guy walking the streets on Broadway, but he understood it as a metaphor for anyone trying to make it. He'd expressed disappointment with the way life was unfolding for him.

"He was recently divorced, estranged from his family, drinking, and involved with drugs a little too much—and yet he was this beautiful soul who we got to know and really love. That song became his signature tune. When you can make that happen, it's very powerful."

"Right Time of the Night" by Jennifer Warnes

"Right Time of the Night" was written by Peter McCann, who released it on his 1977 self-titled album. Jennifer Warnes had a No. 6 hit with the tune in 1977.

"I was out at the beach at Malibu, and it was one of those perfect sunsets," McCann recalled in the Tennessean. "I was there for the entire evening, and the sun went down and the stars came out.

"It was just a beautiful day out there. But one of the things that I didn't do—and it was totally accidental—I didn't mention the beach in the song. I didn't mention anything like that because I think that would have regionalized it.

"Clive Davis, who was heading up Arista Records at the time, he had just signed Jennifer Warnes, and they needed a single for her. He picked the song and got Jim Ed Norman to produce it."

Warnes, however, believed the lyrics were too male-oriented and refused to sing it until McCann wrote a new second verse.

"Jennifer Warnes didn't want to do 'Right Time of the Night,'" said Norman in Producing Country: The Inside Story of Great Recordings.

"I tried to intellectually express why I thought that song could work for her, how it had potential, how it could be done, saying I would do my best to make sure that she got what she wanted. It took several dinners and meals to finally get her to kind of relax and say, 'Okay, okay.'"

"I'm grateful for it, but I didn't pick the song," Warnes said on the Bob Edwards XM Radio show. "It's a mixed feeling to have someone else make the decisions for you, and then of course it's successful because they have the radio operation. What can I say? People love the song."

"I don't think there are too many people who couldn't sing 'Right Time of the Night,'" McCann told the Bridgeport (CT) Post.

"You want a lot of people to record a lot of your songs. You aim for that kind of a reputation. A lot of people think I should be upset because Jennifer had a hit with 'Right Time of the Night,' but it did as much for me as it did for her in terms of reputation."

"Rose Garden" by Lynn Anderson

"Rose Garden" was written in 1967 by Joe South, whose hits included "Down in the Boondocks" by Billy Joe Royal and "Hush" by Deep Purple. South recorded "Rose Garden," as did Royal and Dobie Gray, but none met with major success.

Lynn Anderson was a country singer who was discouraged when she suggested recording the song. "My record producer, Glenn Sutton, was also my husband," Anderson explained in the Texarkana Gazette.

"I had found 'Rose Garden' on a Joe South album and loved it, and I wanted to record it. And right off the bat, Glenn told me that I could not record the song because it was not a girl's song—that the song had some lines in it that a girl just would not sing! Like the line 'I could promise you things like big diamond rings' that a girl would not sing.'

"But later, during a recording session, we ran out of songs to record, so I finally got to record 'Rose Garden.'"

"Glenn sort of raised his eyebrows," Anderson told writer Gene Stout. "But as soon as we started playing it, the guys in the studio said, 'Whoa.' And after the session, we couldn't get them to go home.

"They called their wives and told them to come listen—and then their buddies. Somebody went out and got a six-pack of beer, and somebody else went out for a bottle of champagne. And we stayed in that studio for about three hours after, listening over and over to that song.

"We figured we had a No. 1 country song, but we had no idea that it would do what it did."

"Rose Garden" topped the country charts in 1970 and became a crossover pop hit, reaching No. 3 on the Billboard Hot 100 in 1971.

"It was popular because it touched on emotions," Anderson told the Associated Press in 1987. "I believe that 'Rose Garden' was released at just the right time.

"People were trying to recover from the Vietnam years. The message in the song—that if you just take hold of life and go ahead, you can make something out of nothing—people just took to that."

"Sentimental Lady" by Bob Welch

"Sentimental Lady" was written by guitarist Bob Welch and first recorded for Fleetwood Mac's 1972 album Bare Trees. The Fleetwood Mac version was 4:34 with backing vocals by Christine McVie.

Welch recorded a shortened version of "Sentimental Lady" in 1977 for his solo album, French Kiss. Released as a single, the song was a No. 8 hit.

"The lyric was probably referencing my first wife at the time, Nancy," Welch told Songfacts. "The original placeholder/dummy lyrics for the chorus—before I had 'real' lyrics—were, 'My legs are sticks and my feet are stones.' I have the old songwriting cassette I used, and that's what I'm saying."

The solo version featured Christine McVie and Lindsey Buckingham as backing singers and producers. Buckingham played multilayered guitars, and McVie sang counterpoint vocals.

"The Mac version of 'Sentimental Lady' is not as polished as the solo version," Welch explained in The Penguin Archives.

"That wasn't a necessarily conscious choice, though. Techniques and our own styles had evolved in the five years between the two versions, plus, a lot of the way version two sounds is due to Lindsey B., who produced it, and Fleetwood Mac's engineers Richard Dashut and Ken Caillat.

"The second verse wasn't in the solo version because the record company liked the shorter length of under three minutes; it was better for a single.

"Christine just invented a different counterpoint part for the solo version; it was all her idea. She's great when it comes to vocal parts!"

"She's Gone" by Hall & Oates

Daryl Hall and John Oates wrote "She's Gone," which only reached No. 30 when released by Atlantic Records in 1973. By the time Tavares scored a hit on the R&B charts with the tune, Hall & Oates had moved to RCA Records.

When "Sara Smile" became Hall & Oates' first Top 10 hit, Atlantic re-released Hall & Oates' original, which reached

No. 7 in 1976. Oates told Grantland that the song was inspired in New York's Greenwich Village.

"I had met this girl at three in the morning in a soul food restaurant in the Village called the Pink Tea Cup," Oates recalled.

"I was in there, God knows why, at three in the morning, and in comes this gal, she had a pink tutu and cowboy boots on, and it was December, and I thought that was pretty cool. So we started dating, we kind of hooked up.

"We saw each other a few times, and then I asked her if she wanted to hang out on New Year's Eve, and she said yes. She was supposed to come to my apartment and meet me, and she never showed up.

"As it was getting toward midnight, I finally realized that she wasn't coming, and I just sat down with my guitar and started writing this almost, like, folk song. All it said was 'She's gone, oh oh oh, she's gone' and 'What went wrong?' It was really very simple.

"The next day Daryl came back to the apartment and we sat down, and I said, 'Hey man, you know I got stood up last night, but I wrote this chorus, this hook that's kind of cool.' And I played it for him, and he sat down at the piano, and he immediately started getting into it, and he played the piano part that you hear in the beginning of the song.

"We began to write the verse together. I bet it didn't take more than an hour to write the whole song. We just used very mundane, everyday images to kind of symbolize loneliness and loss, even in the opening line, 'Everybody's high on consolation / everybody's trying to tell me what's right for me,' 'I'm worn as a toothbrush hanging in the stand,' these very simple, lonely images, they're very kind of everyday things that people can relate to but somehow speak on more universal terms.

"I think that's really why the song has connected over the years, because everyone can relate to the idea of loss. We just captured this spirit in some way that has just stood the test of time."

"Snowbird" by Anne Murray

"Snowbird" was Anne Murray's first hit, reaching No. 8 in the US and No. 2 in her native Canada in 1970. "Well, it changed my life," Murray told Udiscover Music.

"It was so exciting. I can still remember watching the charts and, all of a sudden, it was No. 45 with a bullet. And here I was in Nova Scotia, for heaven's sake, so far removed from anything show business. And there it was, climbing up the charts.

"And then, I was in New York City doing these interviews. I didn't know what hit me. It was just a whirlwind. I didn't know what I was doing for about three years."

"Snowbird" was written by Gene MacLellan on Canada's Prince Edward Island. Murray told MacLellan biographer David Sheffield, "Gene told me he wrote the song in 20 minutes when he was walking on a beach in P.E.I. It's so appropriate, the mental picture of Gene—this frail little guy on the beach in the middle of winter, seeing these birds and conjuring up this image."

Murray met MacLellan when they were regulars on the Canadian TV show Singalong Jubilee. "Bill Langstroth was the producer-director on the show, and he introduced me to Gene," Murray explained.

"Bill said, 'You've got to hear these songs. They're so good.' So Gene came up to a conference room, when he sat there with his guitar, and he brought this little tape, and he sat and played.

"I was so taken with his singing, and I was so taken with 'Snowbird.' And I said, 'Well, would it be OK if I took those songs and learned them?' And he said, 'Oh, yes. Sure, you can have them.' So, I walked out of the room with a tape in my hand."

"Snowbird" became a Top 10 crossover country hit, and country music fans became Murray's biggest audience.

"Sometimes When We Touch" by Dan Hill

Canadian singer-songwriter Dan Hill's biggest success was 1978's "Sometimes When We Touch." Hill's lyrics, written in 1973 when he was 19, were paired with music by Barry Mann. Hill wrote the No. 3 hit in an attempt to win the heart of a woman who was dating a photographer and a football player at the same time.

"She was interested in another man, so that was breaking my heart," Hill told ABS-CBN News. "So I thought I needed to write a song that would capture her and win her over—that would be so passionate in a sense that she'd see that I'm the only guy for her.

"I wrote her the song, and I played it over the telephone, and she said, 'That song is just too intense for me. I'm going to the States with the football player.'"

By 1977, Hill's popularity in Canada had not translated into a big US hit. During a meeting with his publisher, ATV Music, ATV's president Sam Trust suggested that Hill collaborate with Mann, the co-writer of smash hits like "You've Lost That Lovin' Feeling" and "On Broadway."

"I agreed to a co-writing session with Barry," Hill wrote in Maclean's. "I met him at the ATV offices on Sunset and Vine.

"'Here, Barry,' pulling a handwritten lyric from the bottom of my guitar case. 'I'm not sure if it's any good. I never wrote any music to it.'

"The latter part was a lie, of course; I was afraid that if he knew I'd written the original music as well, he might think I was handing him a cast-off and take offense. 'If you can do something with it, great. But don't feel any obligation if you hate it.'"

Mann had written the music for "Sometimes When We Touch" by the next day. Hill wrote that Mann doubled up the chorus, requiring Hill to write additional lyrics.

"I realized then that my original music to 'Sometimes' had sounded funereal and turgid, making it impossible for a listener to wade through my chord changes to actually hear and feel the lyrics," wrote Hill.

"But Barry's gripping verse melody—offset by the release of his light, ingeniously sing-songy chorus—gave these same words a kind of soaring majesty that made them instantly memorable."

"Speak to the Sky" by Rick Springfield

Singer-songwriter and multi-instrumentalist Rick Springfield was a member of the popular Australian band Zoot before it broke up in May 1971. Springfield told Screamer magazine that a rock critic aided his decision to go solo.

"One of the writers from the only music magazine over there, Michelle, really pushed me to be a solo artist," said Springfield. "I was just looking for another band, because I thought of myself as a guitar player and a writer. But she pushed me. I don't know if I would've done it on my own."

Springfield's first solo hit Down Under was "Speak to the Sky." Springfield was signed by Capitol Records in the States, where "Speak to the Sky" reached No. 14 in 1972.

"It was very different from what I became known for playing," Springfield explained in the St. Pete Catalyst. "It was kind of a country, almost holy roller kind of song. It's been in prayer books and covered by quite a few artists. It was a good couple of hours, writing that song."

The song was inspired by a tragedy in his family.

"I wrote this song for my mom, because my dad got very sick around that time," said Springfield. "He actually died, and they brought him back, but he was very different after they resuscitated him. He had severe brain damage.

"So I wrote this song about 'if you're in trouble, just speak to the sky, God is there' kind of thing. It was very naive. But my mom had said, 'Why don't you write a nice song?' Because I'd written all these songs she didn't understand.

"So I wrote this nice song for my mom and it became a hit."

"Sweet City Woman" by the Stampeders

The Stampeders—singer-guitarist Rich Dodson, bassist Ronnie King, and drummer Kim Berly—are a Canadian band who reached No. 8 in 1971 with "Sweet City Woman." The banjo-driven track was written by Dodson and introduced to the band at an Ontario club date.

"Rich said, 'I've got this new song,' and he started playing and singing it," Berly recalled in the Penticton Herald. "Ronnie and I began to play along. We got it on about the fourth try. We didn't know if it was going to be a hit, but it was definitely the catchiest thing we had come up with."

"I worked on it off and on for maybe two or three days," Dodson said in Classic Bands.

"It was just a really neat lick. It just came together. It was just a neat little entity. I borrowed a banjo on the way to the studio from a music store. I was just a neat lick, I thought, to play on banjo. It's just magic, a lot of hooks."

"That was one of those miraculous things that just starts and you know right away it's going to be a hit," Berly explained in A Taste of the Kawarthas.

"'Sweet City Woman' was pure pop. The banjo was an afterthought. Rich didn't play banjo, so he just tuned it like a guitar, which has frustrated banjo players for years and years."

"Take Me Home, Country Roads" by John Denver

"Take Me Home, Country Roads" introduced the country to John Denver, who scored a No. 2 hit in 1971. Despite its lyrics about the Blue Ridge Mountains of West Virginia, songwriter Bill Danoff had never been to the Mountain State before writing it.

"I did get the idea riding down a country road in Maryland, but it was the idea of country roads anywhere that inspired the song," Danoff told the Library of Congress, which selected the song for inclusion in the National Recording Registry.

"Driving down that road felt familiar, and I thought that was a feeling everybody could relate to. I repeated 'country roads' over and over for a month or so while working on the tune, and then the first lines came at once out of the blue: 'Almost heaven, West Virginia, Blue Ridge Mountains, Shenandoah River' — all beautiful words.

"It sounded good to me, and I never seriously thought of changing it."

Danoff and his wife and songwriting partner Taffy Nivert were working on the song when their friend, John Denver, visited them in Washington, DC.

"When John came over, and Taffy and I sang 'Country Roads' for him, he basically flipped out," recalled Danoff. "He said, 'Wow, that's a hit! Did you record that?'

"And I said, 'No, we don't have a record deal.' And he said, 'Well, I got a record deal and I'm doing an album now. Can we do it on my album together?'

"I said the song's not quite finished. I had the whole melody, Taffy had harmonies, we had the chorus just the way it is now, and the first verse just the way it is now. I had different words in the second verse, and I did not have a lyric for the bridge, the 'I hear her voice' part. So, the song pretty much sounded like it does, and John was very enthusiastic. He said, 'Well, let's finish it.'

"So we stayed up all night, and we shouted out words 'til we'd written another second verse and filled in the bridge lyric. By 6:30 in the morning, we had the song that you know today.

"We sang it all together the first time, and we all knew that we had something special. It sounded like a hit to us."

Danoff played acoustic guitar at the recording session but at first was not pleased with the result. "I thought, 'Oh, my God. There's way too much echo on that,' he told NPR.

"I loved the song, but I thought we'd blown the record. And millions of other people didn't agree."

"The Closer I Get to You" by Roberta Flack with Donny Hathaway

In 1972, Roberta Flack and Donny Hathaway collaborated on a self-titled album of duets that included "Where Is the Love." Five years later, the singers scored a No. 2 hit with "The Closer I Get to You" from Flack's album Blue Lights in the Basement.

Hathaway suffered from severe bouts of clinical depression, which often forced him to be hospitalized. Flack, a long-time friend who attended Howard University with Hathaway, asked the soul singer to join her to help.

"I love Donny," Flack told Songwriter Universe in 2020. "Donny is a musical genius, and I don't use that word often or lightly.

"Donny had his struggles through the years, but when he sat at the piano and sang for and with me, it was as if nothing was wrong—he sang and played and created magnificently.

"Members of my band—James Mtume and Reggie Lucas—wrote 'The Closer I Get to You' not as a duet, originally. I wanted to have it rewritten as a duet as a way to help Donny, who was suffering from severe depression at the time.

"He wasn't able to come from Chicago to New York for the recording, but did his part of the song in Chicago, and it was later mixed with my vocal. When I listen to my recordings, it's one of the most beautiful yet most painful songs for me to hear to this day."

"I tried to reach out to Donny," Flack explained in Jet in 1979. "That's how we managed to do the song we did last year.

"I felt this need because I didn't know what to do. I couldn't save him, I knew he was sick. But I knew when he sat down at that piano and sang for me, it was like it was eight or nine years ago because he sang and played his ass off."

When Blue Lights in the Basement was released, Flack told Classic Soul that she kept the songs, including "The Closer I Get to You," short to encourage radio airplay.

"We've had to be more conscious of the limits because, frankly, people won't get to hear those mammoth cuts," said Flack. "Radio stations won't play them.

"Take the cut, 'The Closer I Get to You,' which we did with Donny Hathaway. You should really hear that one in its entirety! It's about eight or nine minutes long, and when we first finished it, and I played it to a few people, they really dug it.

"If you heard the whole thing, it would really blow your mind because the end is just incredible—the ad-libs and stuff that go on between us. Believe me, I didn't want it to be edited, and if ever there's a way of releasing that full version, I hope it happens!"

"The Morning After" by Maureen McGovern

In March 1972, 20th Century Fox songwriters Al Kasha and Joel Hirschhorn were given a challenge: They had one day to write the love theme of the film The Poseidon Adventure. The pair worked through the night and presented a song titled, "Why Must There Be a Morning After?"

Executive producer Irwin Allen loved the song but asked that the title be changed to "The Morning After" with the lyric "There's got to be a morning after" to project a more positive message.

"The Morning After" was recorded by Renee Armand, with Carol Linley lip-synching to it in the film. When the song won Best Original Song at the Academy Awards, Russ Regan, head of 20th Century Records, looked for someone to record the song for the singles market.

"I was part of a small band with my husband as the drummer," Ohio's Maureen McGovern told Goldmine. "We played at the Holiday Inns and Ramada Inns in the area.

"We recorded demos, sent them to labels, and got a 'yes' from 20th Century. Russ Regan heard something that the other labels didn't and signed me to 20th Century in October of 1972, and in November, we recorded 'The Morning After.'"

Kasha and Hirshhorn presented McGovern's version to Allen. "He was very shaken by it," recalled Kasha. "He had never heard of this girl in his life. He asked us what we thought of it, and we told him we loved it. We weren't just being Monday morning quarterbacks—we thought she captured the song beautifully."

"The single didn't hit initially," said McGovern. "After the Academy Award nomination, my single version received attention from easy listening stations who were curious. Then the requests built up and finally became a big hit and won the Oscar. It spent two weeks at number one late that summer and went gold."

"It struck a chord of hope," explained Kasha. "It can be read as a personalized kind of song. It could be read as a love song. It could be read as a song for a person who's on alcohol or some kind of drug, 'There's got to be a morning after,' meaning getting through the night.

"It's just a great song of hope."

"The Night Chicago Died" by Paper Lace

Paper Lace was a British band whose only international hit was "The Night Chicago Died." The fictional account of a shootout between Al Capone's mob and the Chicago police topped the charts in 1974.

"The Night Chicago Died" was written by Peter Callander and Mitch Murray, who had previously scored with "Billy, Don't Be a Hero." Murray explained the writers' liberal approach to history in Songfacts.

"My writing partner, Peter Callander, and I are both British, and it's true, we'd never been to Chicago at the time we wrote the song," said Murray.

"Having been brought up on a tasty diet of American gangster movies, the term 'East Side' usually meant the seamy side of a city. Of course, looking back, it was used about New York, not Chicago.

"We (actually, I mostly blame Peter because he had the last words on lyrics while I had the last word on the tunes) were obviously a little careless with our research, as we were when we wrote about Al Capone fighting the 'forces of the law.' I really don't think that ever happened; apparently, the cops were nearly all on Capone's payroll.

"The song was certainly a work of fiction, and as such, perhaps we should have used fictional gangster names. Still, it's hard to have regrets when your song is No. 1 in the USA."

"The Streak" by Ray Stevens

Streaking was popular in the early 1970s, originated by college students running naked around campus. Singer-songwriter Ray Stevens spotted a Newsweek article about the fad while on a flight to Los Angeles.

"It was a little bitty article about a college student who took off his clothes and ran through a crowd," Stevens told Billboard. "The article called it 'streaking' and I said it had to be a great idea for a song.

"I made some notes, and when I got to my hotel room, I made some more notes. When I got home from the trip, I dashed out a few lines. I intended to finish it whenever I could find the time.

"I didn't know it was going to be such a big fad. One morning, I woke up and it was all over the news.

Everywhere you turned, people were talking about streakers. So I built a fire under myself and went into the studio."

"I was polishing it when we were recording it in the studio," Stevens recalled in the Tennessean. "We'd do a playback and I would say, 'Nah, I'm going to change that.'

"By the time we got through with it, though, it was right there. We made an acetate, that was back in the day! 'The Streak' was 1974. We sent it to the Top 40 station here in Nashville and said, 'Test this for us, will ya? Do us a favor?'

"They said sure. They played it and their switchboard lit up. They called us back and said, 'This is a monster!' So we got it out as soon as we could."

"The Streak" spent three weeks at the top of the Billboard chart in 1974.

"There were 15 other streaking records already on the market by the time I got mine out," said Stevens. "There ended up being 35–40 streaking records altogether. Stores were setting up sections for the 'streaks of the week.' I got the jump on everybody, I think, by getting lucky and reading that article."

"This Masquerade" by George Benson

"This Masquerade" was written and first recorded by Leon Russell for his 1972 album Carney. Helen Reddy and the Carpenters followed with their covers. Singer-guitarist George Benson reached No. 10 in 1976 with his recording of "This Masquerade," which featured Jorge Dalto on piano. Benson was introduced to the song by his producer, Tommy LiPuma.

"I ended up working with producers who had great respect for songs. Tommy LiPuma was one," Benson said in DIY

Musician. "I said, 'Man, who's this Leon Russell? Never heard of him!'

"And I hadn't listened to it yet. So he sent it to me again, and one more time. And what made me change my mind was my piano player at the time, Jorge Dalto—he's long gone now—but he brought his wife to my new house, which I'd just bought, and she said, 'Oh, that's my favorite song. That's Leon Russell.'

"I said, 'How can this person know more about the music business than me? If this guy's a star, how come I don't know him? Maybe I better learn this, ya know?'"

Benson recorded "This Masquerade" for his 1976 album, Breezin', and it became the first big hit of his career.

"I agreed to do one take to see what happened," Benson recalled on the Rhino website. "That one take was the only take ever recorded by me.

"Tommy made a statement in the studio which turned out to be the truth: 'We could be here all day tracking, and it will never get better than this.' He immediately took the recording to Warner Bros. All the executives were in a high-level meeting in which he broke in.

"He played 'This Masquerade' fresh out of the studio to this group of hit-makers, and they all fell in love with it immediately. When asked who was the artist, he said George Benson. They were shocked, as they only thought of me as a guitar player until then."

"Time Passages" by Al Stewart

"Time Passages" was British singer-songwriter Al Stewart's follow-up to his 1976 debut hit, "Year of the Cat." Arista Records signed Stewart on the strength of "Year of the Cat."

"It was the first serious money that I saw in my life," Stewart recalled in Songwriter Universe. "Clive Davis was running it.

"He said, 'I want some midtempo ballads—120 beats per minute with a saxophone on it.' And I thought, I don't know what he's talking about. I'm a songwriter—what is this beats per minute nonsense? So basically with 'Time Passages,' I just cloned 'Year of the Cat.'"

Guitarist Peter White co-wrote "Time Passages." White told Goldmine how the song came together.

"'Time Passages' was put together in late September 1977 in Al's apartment in West Hollywood, near the Roxy Theatre on Sunset Boulevard where a year later we would debut this song in concert," said White.

"I had played the intro piano figure to Al earlier that year, and he had said, 'Let's make a song out of that.' So, late summer 1977, I flew into Los Angeles from New Jersey, where I was vacationing with friends, and staying at the Chateau Marmont, I would walk down Sunset Boulevard to his apartment, where we worked.

"Al came up with the verse and chorus, which were based on my intro piano figure, and I came up with the chords for the bridge and the instrumental extravaganza that followed."

"Time Passages" reached No. 7 in late 1978, but Stewart maintains he does not like the tune.

"I'll tell you a funny story," Stewart said in Acoustic Storm. "I have never really cared for that song. I know it was a big hit and all that. It was just one of those things where the record company asked me to write something that sounded like 'Year of the Cat' and we ended up doing that.

"But I didn't realize truly how bad a song it was until one day I was in an elevator and I was listening to what I thought was Muzak. About 30 seconds went by, and I finally began to recognize it and said to myself, 'This sounds pretty horrible.'

"Then, horror of horrors, I heard my voice come on; it actually was the record. So I'm thinking, 'Oh my God, what have I done? This is terrible!'

"Hopefully, in the last 25 years, I've redeemed myself with other things, but 'Time Passages' has just never thrilled me."

"Too Much, Too Little, Too Late" by Johnny Mathis and Deniece Williams

"Too Much, Too Little, Too Late" was a comeback for Johnny Mathis, whose last No. 1 hit was 1957's "Chances Are." Mathis and R&B singer Deniece Williams topped the charts in 1978 with the song penned by Nat Kipner and John Vallins.

To jumpstart his career, Mathis' producer, Jack Gold, and CBS Records A&R executive Mike Dilbeck suggested Williams as a partner on Mathis' first duet.

"Jack had heard of Deniece and her success and knew how clever she was in the studio with background voices," Mathis explained in Billboard.

"I grew up on R&B, jazz, and classical music. So when we decided to try something different, we knew Deniece was big in the R&B area, so I said, 'Maybe we can get some of the R&B diehards to listen to some of my music.' We decided the best way was to get someone who was already accepted in that area and see what happens."

"I remember my manager saying the record company wants to know if you're interested in singing with Johnny Mathis," Williams told Billboard.

"I said, 'Are you kidding? Do I want to sing with Johnny Mathis?' I was devastated. I couldn't believe that I was going to get a chance to sing with Johnny.

"And then I didn't believe that they would use the record. I thought, well, they probably won't use this, so I said, 'Can I have a tape for me?'"

Williams recalled in Blues & Soul magazine that "the vibes were great" during the recording session.

"It was particularly interesting, because it was a first for both of us," said Williams. "Neither had ever done a 'duet' per se, and it seemed like we just fell right into the groove."

"It was just so much fun working with Johnny," said Williams. "He's such a gentleman. I've never met a more humble spirit in someone who had every right not to be humble. He really taught me the value of humility in the midst of your success."

"Torn Between Two Lovers" by Mary MacGregor

"Torn Between Two Lovers" was written by Peter Yarrow of Peter, Paul & Mary and Phillip Jarrell. The song about a love triangle was a No. 1 hit in 1977.

Yarrow said on the Peter, Paul & Mary website that his wife inspired the tune.

"I was asking Mary Beth what I should write about," Yarrow explained, "and she said, 'Why don't you write a song about being, like Dr. Zhivago, in the middle of two love relationships and loving both people?'

"Phil Jarrell was going through a really difficult time with the breakup of his marriage and was only semi-there in a lot of ways. He was experiencing a lot of pain. A lot of the lyric was written for the verses while Phil was there, but the chorus actually was written after he left, as was the final melody."

"I auditioned and got a gig singing backup vocals for Peter Yarrow," Mary MacGregor told James E. Aarons. "He was on a summer solo tour, and we traveled, mostly by bus, through the south and southeastern US.

"Peter had written some songs that he thought a woman should sing, so we stopped in Muscle Shoals, Alabama, where I recorded them for him. 'Torn Between Two Lovers' was one of those songs.

"When Barry Beckett and I decided to co-produce Mary MacGregor," said Yarrow, "she didn't really want to record the song. She said that she just didn't feel she could identify with the person and the message that was being said because she wouldn't do that."

"A lot of people are torn between two lovers, or have been, or will be," MacGregor told Billboard.

"I think it's a real implausible situation. A lady who wants to have her cake and eat it, too. At the time I recorded the song, I was married and people thought I'd written it and wanted to know if *I* was 'torn.' It was real aggravating for me, although the success that it had was definitely not."

"Undercover Angel" by Alan O'Day

Alan O'Day was a successful singer-songwriter who wrote "Angie Baby," a No. 1 hit for Helen Reddy in 1974. Warner Bros. Music created Pacific Records in 1977 for their songwriters who also performed. O'Day was the first artist signed to the label. His debut single was "Undercover Angel."

O'Day told Classic Bands that he began to write the lyrics before he had a song title.

"I started writing the song, 'Crying on my pillow, lonely in my bed, then I heard a voice beside me, and she softly said, Wonder is your night light.' I get this idea, a little bit like 'Angie Baby,' that it was an out-of-body experience or something spiritual or mystical as well as sexual, but I didn't know what the main point of the song was.

"Then it was searching for a title. That's when 'Undercover Angel' came together for me.

"I love the word 'undercover.' Looking back on it, I think the word angel was invoked because of Charlie's Angels, the TV show, but I didn't really know that then. I just put the two words together, and I loved what it said."

"Undercover Angel" was a No. 1 smash in 1977 before O'Day had a chance to record an album. "'Undercover Angel' is kind of a corny song, and it's kind of a sexy song, and it's kind of an infantile song, and it sold two million copies," O'Day told Soft Rock Café.

"I think it's a good song, and I am proud of its success. It was banned in Peoria, Illinois, as being too sexual, and I've always worn that as a badge of pride [*laughs*]. I had no illusions that I was creating great art. I've just always loved the idea of the little three-minute movie."

"It's wonderful when you find out what feels right," O'Day said in Super Seventies, "and then it also feels right to other people. That's a songwriter's dream."

"United We Stand" by the Brotherhood of Man

"United We Stand" by the Brotherhood of Man was written by British songwriters Tony Hiller and Peter Simons, the pseudonym for group member Johnny Goodison. "I wrote

'United We Stand' in 1969 with my dear departed friend, Johnny Goodison," Hiller told Songfacts.

"Believe it or not, I had two jobs at that time—I was General Professional Manager of an American music publishing company, Mills Music, and I was also a record producer for Decca Records UK. I produced the record at Decca Studios, London.

The young Reg Dwight, who later became Elton John, worked for Hiller at Mills Music. "I didn't know he could write then," Hiller said in The Independent, "but he was always singing and I asked him to make the original demo of 'United We Stand.'

"At the recording, I had great musicians, wonderful arrangement, terrific engineer, and the exceptional voices of the Brotherhood of Man, which I had founded and put together."

Besides Goodison, the Brotherhood of Man included an all-star lineup of British session singers: Tony Burrows, Sue Glover, and Sunny Leslie, along with writer Roger Greenaway.

"I was so honored and lucky to have worked with such a wonderful array of talent," said Hiller. "When I played back the recording I had made, there was thunderous applause in the studio. We all knew that there was magic in the air.

"The inspiration for the song was definitely in the title, 'United We Stand.' It was during the time of Flower Power, the Vietnam War, the founding of lots of movements, including gay liberation and civil rights. It was, in fact, immediately taken up and used as the rallying call for the US Democratic Party presidential campaign."

The popularity of "United We Stand" as an international anthem surprised Hiller.

"I never intended for 'United We Stand' to be an anthem," said Hiller. "It was written as a love song, but for some reason, people took a shine to it and have used it for all sorts of purposes.

"Often when people want to show solidarity, they sing 'United We Stand.' I'm very proud of that, but I know it has also been played at a mafia funeral."

"Vincent" by Don McLean

Don McLean wrote "Vincent" as a tribute to Vincent Van Gogh, the Dutch painter who created The Starry Night in 1889. Van Gogh painted the swirling Starry Night after committing himself to an asylum in France.

McLean wrote "Vincent" in 1970 while living in Massachusetts. "I had a job singing in the school system, playing my guitar in classrooms," McLean recalled in The Telegraph.

"I was sitting on the veranda one morning, reading a biography of Van Gogh, and suddenly I knew I had to write a song arguing that he wasn't crazy. He had an illness and so did his brother Theo.

"This makes it different, in my mind, to the garden variety of 'crazy'—because he was rejected by a woman. So I sat down with a print of Starry Night and wrote the lyrics out on a paper bag."

Released on McLean's 1971 American Pie album, "Vincent" peaked at No. 12 on the Billboard chart in 1972. McLean told Forbes that at first, he struggled with the lyrics.

"I thought, 'Since the brother and Vincent had similar illnesses, wouldn't it be interesting to write that story?' But how am I going to do it? I mean, one man singing to another about his art and death could be really stupid if you didn't find a way to make the song beautiful and elegant. I like beautiful things, and have a dash of elegance myself.

"Then it hit me. All I had to do was look at Starry Night. When I did, the painting wrote the song. I don't do the melody first, then tack the words on. I just sing into a tape recorder, and the song comes right out of me."

"Wake Up Everybody" by Harold Melvin & the Blue Notes

"Wake Up Everybody" is a prime example of the 1970s Philadelphia soul sound. Harold Melvin & the Blue Notes, with lead vocals by Teddy Pendergrass, scored a No. 12 hit with the tune in 1976.

"Wake Up Everybody" was written by John Whitehead, Gene McFadden, and Victor Carstarphen and produced by Kenny Gamble and Leon Huff. "We helped them in many ways to write the song, but it was a fantastic collaboration for all of us to work on together," Gamble told Wax Poetics in 2021.

"With Teddy Pendergrass being a feature on that album, it was another thing that gave the group a wide range of talents."

"Wake Up Everybody" was recorded in Philadelphia's Sigma Sound. "We recorded 'Wake Up Everybody' in Studio B," said Gamble.

"We were kind of close in there, because that was a smaller studio than Studio A upstairs. But we kept going in that studio. We started to move it upstairs, but when we did, we said, 'No, let's keep it here because it feels good.'

"Just the band was in there. Teddy might have walked in later on, just to make sure the tempo and everything was right. We very rarely recorded live vocals with the artists and the band, because the microphones would be open and you would get the bleed-in from the band on the artist's mic."

Gamble explained the song's significance 45 years after its release. "That song is self-explanatory, because it is the way the world is right now. The bottom line of all this stuff here is that if you don't take care of your young, then who will take care of you? We must take care of our young and train them and teach them.

"Education is the number one thing. It always has been and always will be. We've got to teach our young. We've got to teach them how to survive and how to deal with one another so that they can survive, because otherwise, they won't survive.

"People had to and still have to wake up. I remember the day that we set foot in that studio, and when I heard them chords, I said, 'Man, that's it. This is going to be a *monster*.'"

"We're All Alone" by Rita Coolidge

In 1971, Rita Coolidge sang backing vocals and arranged and directed the other backing singers on Boz Scaggs' albums Moments and Boz Scaggs & Band. Coolidge was quick to agree when her record company suggested she cover "We're All Alone" from the Scaggs album Silk Degrees.

"When I was with A&M Records, it was like a family," Coolidge told Spencer Leigh.

"I would visit Herb Alpert and Jerry Moss, and it was a very open, communicative group of people. One day, I was in Jerry Moss' office, and he said that the Boz Scaggs album Silk Degrees was in a million homes and there was a song on it that was perfect for a woman to sing.

"He said, 'It's called "We're All Alone" and as he's not doing it as a single, I think you ought to record it.'"

"I had the record," Coolidge said in Goldmine. "I had played Silk Degrees probably 150 times by then, and I knew every word. So by the time Jerry brought me into the office and said, 'I think a girl should be singing "We're All Alone," I said, 'You'll get no argument from me. I want to sing all of Boz's songs.'"

Coolidge recorded "We're All Alone" for her 1977 album Anytime . . . Anywhere. Coolidge explained in the Aquarian how she applied her style to other writers' songs.

"I was always in control of the songs that I sing," said Coolidge. "No one is going to make me sing something I don't want to sing.

"I think that was my fourth album with producer David Anderle. He and I had established a really great relationship. Booker T. Jones was part of that record as well.

"I always felt that there were songs sung by guys that needed to be sung by women. One of those songs was 'We're All Alone,' which was written by Boz Scaggs. I gave those songs new life.

"Just the fact that I'm singing it and Boz is not gives it a whole different spin because it's a woman singing a love song about being alone with her lover. As far as the orchestration, I think we recorded it in the same key that Boz did.

"Booker was on board then as co-producer, and we wanted it to literally have a shimmer to it—with the strings—and make it elegant and beautiful so it could reflect the perfection of the lyrics and the music that Boz wrote.

"He did an incredible job with that song. It's just timeless! When you've got a great song and you've got a great team and I happen to be the singer, I don't know where the magic comes in.

"I think it's a combination of all of those things. Just having the right people together and the right song in the studio with the right musicians. There's no formula. We're all just trying to do it right."

"We're All Alone" was a No. 7 hit in 1977. "I was very pleased that Rita had a huge success with it," Scaggs told Record Collector.

"She gave the song stature and her version is more in the spirit in which it was written than anyone else's."

"We've Only Just Begun" by the Carpenters

"It had all the romantic beginnings of a bank commercial," is the way lyricist Paul Williams described his song "We've Only Just Begun" in Songfacts. Williams and composer Roger Nichols wrote the song as an ad for Crocker Bank in California.

"There was actually a wonderful writer named Tony Asher who wrote for this ad agency," said Williams, "and he'd had a skiing accident and he broke his arm, so he couldn't write or play the piano or whatever. So he suggested Roger Nichols and I as replacements to write this ad.

"The ad agency called us and said, 'Look, we're going to show a young couple getting married, driving off into the sunset, and it's going to say, "You've got a long way to go, we'd like to help you get there to the Crocker Bank."'

"And I went, Okay, what rhymes with Crocker? Crocker what? To write a jingle. And they said very specifically, 'No, we don't want a jingle.'

"What they asked for is what we would today call a music video. It was going to show a young couple getting married, driving off into the sunset. After the ceremony, the first kiss and all. So Roger and I wrote the song that would play over that."

Freddie Allen first recorded the song to little notice, and Williams provided the vocals for the commercial.

"It was a very effective commercial," Richard Carpenter told NPR. "And I heard that a couple of times, and I knew darn well it was by Nichols and Williams 'cause I recognized Paul's voice. And I thought, it's a hit."

The Carpenters—keyboardist Richard and drummer Karen Carpenter, who sang lead—were looking for a follow-up to their debut hit, 1970's "(They Long to Be) Close to You," and believed they'd found it in "We've Only Just Begun," which reached No. 2 that year.

"It became the wedding song of a generation, my goodness," said Richard. "It worked very well for our harmonies as well as Karen's lead. And it was a nice combination of softer pop, at times, and then had a little more edge to it.

"It's an arranger's dream, that song."

"Which Way You Goin' Billy?" by the Poppy Family

"Which Way You Goin' Billy?" was a No. 2 hit for the Poppy Family in 1970. The Canadian band was primarily singer-songwriter Terry Jacks, whose "Seasons in the Sun" was a No. 1 smash in 1974, and his wife, Susan, who performed lead vocals.

"Originally, the song was called 'Which Way You Goin' Buddy?' Terry had written it for a guy to sing," Susan told Goldmine.

"Mike Campbell, who used to be on Music Hop with me, which was the Canadian national TV show that I was on since I was 15, ended up singing it. It was relatively early in our marriage, and I didn't want to hurt Terry's feelings, but the song was about a guy asking another guy which way he was going and if he could go too, and I thought, what a wimp!

"I loved the melody. I thought it was awesome, and I suggested that he write it for a woman. It would be more commercial and more of a woman's song. So Terry did."

"Buddy Holly was my idol, and it was written as, 'Which way you goin', Buddy?' Terry recalled in Songfacts. "I had the melody of the chorus in my mind a few years before I'd written the song, and I was trying to figure something out, and I couldn't figure it out. Nothing was working.

"I had this great chorus: 'You are my soul, babe, my heart and my soul.' You know, 'You are my whole, baby, my heart.' It was a real infectious chorus, but I didn't know where to take the thing.

"It was in 1969, and I had been reading about all these guys going to Vietnam and leaving their women behind in Seattle, and I knew somebody down there that was doing that. I thought, 'Wow, that must be awful.'

"These guys go, and their wives or girlfriends wouldn't know whether they were coming back. That's quite a deal, going to war over there, and it was such a stupid war. So I said, 'That's what I'm going to write about: this woman that's left behind. Which way you going, Billy? Can I go, too?'

"I didn't know which name to use after 'Which way you going.' I had no clue. But one of my favorite groups in Canada was a group called the Beau-Marks. They were out of Montreal, and had one big hit in the States called 'Clap Your Hands.' But my favorite song of theirs was called 'Billy, Billy Went a Walkin'.' It was a really neat song.

"I thought, 'Which way you goin' . . . ah, Billy!' That'd be a great name."

"We went in the studio and recorded it," said Terry. "Susan sang it perfect, but it didn't have the feel I wanted. It's a very sad song, and it was done really well.

"I remember going home with her that night—we were married—and saying, 'There's something wrong. I don't like it.' And she was saying, 'Oh, I think it's fine.' I said, 'No.'

"Because as a producer, I didn't figure it caught that emotion that I wanted. It was too happy-sounding. It was really well done, but it was too happy.

"I argued with her, and finally, I said, 'Look, I'm going to cut it again. We've still got the track, I want to cut it again.' So the next day we went in and she did it first take, because she was so tired and she was so worn out, she captured the feel. It fit the song."

"Wildfire" by Michael Martin Murphey

"Wildfire" tells the story of a Nebraska woman who freezes to death in a blizzard while trying to find her escaped pony, Wildfire. "Wildfire" was written by Michael Martin Murphey and Larry Cansler. The song was a No. 3 hit for Murphey in 1975.

The song came to Murphey as he was working on The Ballad of Calico, a concept album for Kenny Rogers about a ghost town in California. "I was living in the mountains in California," Murphey told The Boot.

"I would drive down to Larry's apartment in Los Angeles and sleep on his floor, because we would work, sometimes, 22 hours a day on the album.

"The night 'Wildfire' came to me, Larry went to bed, and I went to sleep in a sleeping bag on the floor. I dreamed the song in its entirety. I woke up and pounded on Larry's door and said, 'Can you come down and help me with this song?' His wife got up and made us coffee, and we finished it in two or three hours.

"We were working on my album Blue Sky—Night Thunder at the time, and my producer Bob Johnson said, 'I don't see how that song will fit in with the rest of the material for that album.' I asked him if I could record it as an album cut, because I felt very strongly about it.

"We recorded the song at Caribou Ranch in Colorado," said Murphey. "After we recorded the song, Bob said, 'You know, it came out better than I thought it would. Let's play it for the kitchen staff here and see what they think.'

"They loved it, so Bob said, 'Okay, we'll release it as the first single.' It came out, took off in Chicago and Milwaukee, and public demand made it a hit, which proves that those of us in music have no clue about anything when it comes to what will be a hit song."

"Year of the Cat" by Al Stewart

Scottish singer-songwriter Al Stewart does not write stereotypical pop songs. His compositions are often complex; short stories are set to music woven with historical references. In John Davies' book Lyrics and Limericks, Stewart said that content is most important to him.

"Content is its raison d'être rather than style. So what I like in a song, and I think I'm in a minority here because most people don't care, but what I want is original content.

"In other words, I want a song to be about something that a song hasn't been about before, and I want it to be written in language which is different from the normal run-of-the-mill pop music language. These are the two priorities when I write a song."

Stewart explained that he usually writes the music first, even before he comes up with the song's title. He often writes four or five different sets of lyrics per song.

"What usually comes first is an idea, like I'm going to make this about the Hungarian Revolution, for example. Then I write the music, and then I fill in the lyrics."

That's how Stewart wrote 1976's "Year of the Cat." The lyrics tell the story of a tourist's romantic adventure with a woman he met in a marketplace.

Inspired by a piano riff by his co-writer, Peter Wood, Stewart first wrote the song as "Foot of the Stage" after attending a performance by Tony Hancock, a British comedian who suffered from depression.

Stewart told Neville Judd in Al Stewart: True Life Adventures of a Folk Troubadour that Hancock shared his pain with the audience that night.

"He came on stage and he said, 'I don't want to be here. I'm just totally pissed off with my life. I'm a complete loser. This is stupid. I don't know why I don't just end it all right here.'

"And they all laughed because this was the character he played . . . this sort of down-and-out character. And I looked at him and I thought, 'Oh my God, He means it. This is for real.'"

When Hancock committed suicide in 1968, Stewart decided he did not want to take advantage of the tragedy. Weaving together the discovery of a Vietnamese astrology book opened to the Year of the Cat, and a man's story about meeting a woman in North Africa, Stewart abandoned the Hancock tale and wrote "Year of the Cat."

In January 1976, Stewart started to record his next album. Until then, Stewart had been an interesting but largely unknown folk rock artist. For the new LP, he teamed with producer Alan Parsons, who helped create a new sound for Stewart.

In a radio interview, Parsons explained how he introduced Stewart to a more jazz-flavored style.

"He always tended to base his music around acoustic instruments, mainly because of his folk background. In fact, the only departure from acoustic instruments at this point was to use the electric guitar up front, in solos, etc.

"But while we were making Al's next album, I made a suggestion to use an old friend of mine, Phil Kenzie, to put a sax solo on the LP's title track. And Al said he'd never heard a sax in his music before, but kind of went along with the idea. And the result was a song which virtually broke Al worldwide: 'Year of the Cat.'"

The single reached No. 8 on the Billboard chart in 1977 and has become a classic rock radio standard. Stewart told Pause & Play that after recording "Year of the Cat," he knew his new jazzy approach would work.

"I thought it was pretty good. I had finished it at nine o'clock in the morning, and I was living in an apartment in West Hollywood, and I had been in the studio all night with Alan Parsons mixing this thing. And I brought it back, and I couldn't go to bed.

"I had not heard it on my home system; it's one thing to listen to a record in a studio because everything sounds great through big speakers, but I wanted to listen to it through tiny little speakers.

"I remember putting it on at nine in the morning for one more time, then around ten in the morning I thought 'This sounds pretty damn good' and I went to sleep."

But Stewart says the album's success didn't immediately change his life for the better.

"The record was so expensive to make, and because of all the promo tours we did, I think it personally cost me a quarter of a million dollars. You had to pay the record company back; you had to pay the producer.

"It worked out that years later, during the period when I was having successful records, I basically broke even on the entire thing. Whereas years later, when I was just going out with an acoustic guitar and wasn't really doing records anymore, you made money. So go figure."

"You and Me Against the World" by Helen Reddy

"You and Me Against the World" was originally written by singer-songwriter Paul Williams and keyboardist Kenny Ascher as a gag song. Williams told Songfacts that he and Ascher were in London trading silly lyrics when they realized they may have stumbled onto a hit.

"We went to England to do a television show. Kenny was a member of my band," said Williams. "And when we got there, there was a problem with the work permits, so the guys in my band couldn't play. I had to use local musicians.

"So Kenny's sitting around with nothing to do in a hotel in London. We're sitting there, and we're having a few drinks, because that's what I did in those days.

"We're sitting around and we're talking about writers, and we all love Cole Porter and a certain kind of writer and all. And we started talking about Harry Nilsson and Randy

Newman.

"So Kenny and I wrote this little song: 'Do you love me, babe, do you love me not? Let's decide in the morning, not now. Boy, you don't like Shuman, or Randy Newman, Nilsson ain't your cup of tea.' It was really kind of a cute little song.

"Kenny's sitting at the piano, turned to me, and he said, 'If that was on an album . . .' and he played the intro to what became 'You and Me Against the World.' And I just looked at him when he finished the intro and sang, 'You and me against the world,' and he hit another chord, and I went, 'Sometimes it feels like you and me against the world.'"

Williams recorded "You and Me Against the World" for his 1974 album Here Comes Inspiration. In her book The Woman I Am: A Memoir, Helen Reddy explained that she found the lyrics "too paternalistic" for a woman to sing. Reddy interpreted it as a mother singing to her child.

Reddy released "You and Me Against the World" on her album Love Song for Jeffrey. The single reached No. 9 in 1974.

"The best part of being a songwriter—beyond being able to make a living at it—is what I call the 'heart payment' of a song," Williams explained.

"That's when somebody comes up after a concert and says, 'My mom was a single mom, and "You and Me Against the World" was a really important song to us.'"

"You Light Up My Life" by Debby Boone

It was difficult to escape hearing "You Light Up My Life" in 1977. It was the title song of a popular film by producer and songwriter Joe Brooks. In the film, actress Didi Conn lip synched a recording by Kasey Cisyk, which was included on the soundtrack album.

"You Light Up My Life" became a monster hit when Curb Records head Mike Curb asked Debby Boone, the daughter of Pat Boone, to record it. "You Light Up My Life" topped the Billboard chart for 10 consecutive weeks in 1977.

"I came home to my parents' house and my mother said Mike Curb had brought a cassette of this song they wanted me to record," Boone recalled in the Spectrum.

"At that point, I had only performed with the family, so I was shocked because we hadn't talked about me doing anything on my own. But I was pleased when I heard this lovely song, and my parents were supportive when I flew to New York to record it."

Brooks commanded the session and insisted Boone strictly follow Cisyk's version.

"When I did the original recording, Joe wanted it to sound exactly like the film version," said Boone. "I had absolutely no artistic freedom about how long to hold the notes or with the melody."

Boone told Pop Culture Classics that people have told her about the connection the song has had in their lives. "Many, many people, this was sung at their wedding," said Boone.

"Some people at funerals. The song has gotten people through some really tough times.

"Whenever I sing the song, you can feel, in the room, people having an emotional, physical response to it, and it's taking them somewhere special in their lives. It's a really incredible thing to be connected to a song that does that for people."

"It wasn't a Christian song," Boone told Billboard, "although many people thought it was. However, mainly because the lyrics really lent themselves to how I felt about my relationship with the Lord, that's the way I chose to sing it. I never really thought anyone would know."

"Young Hearts Run Free" by Candi Staton

Producer and songwriter David Crawford wanted to work with soul singer Candi Staton for years when they met at Warner Bros. Records. The label had opened a disco division and Crawford saw an opportunity.

"He wanted to get into a more spiritual realm, and asked me where I was in my life," Staton recalled in The Guardian.

"I told him I was trying to get out of a really bad relationship; this guy was threatening me and telling me that if I ever left him, he'd kill me or kill my kids. I was so fearful.

"David poured all this into writing 'Young Hearts Run Free.' He had a lot of great songs, but said they were album cuts, not hits. But when he came up with 'Young Hearts Run Free,' I instantly loved it.

"I heard the music first, then he sang it to me once and gave me the lyric sheet. Then I sang it in one take. I pleaded with him to let me do it again, and he said, "You can, but I've got it."

"As an artist, the first take contains the raw emotion. The hurt in my voice is real. I was singing my life."

"Young Hearts Run Free" reached No. 20 on the pop chart and topped the Billboard Hot Soul Singles chart in 1976.

"In my life, I had fallen into a well, and the song is me trying to give advice to younger women: Don't have babies with him, because he'll be busy loving every other woman he can, but you'll be stuck.

"Know that there's a future behind every choice, and you're not always going to like it. The song is telling them to run free. So many women know exactly what I'm talking about."

"(You're) Having My Baby" by Paul Anka

When "(You're) Having My Baby" topped the charts in 1974, it marked 15 years since Paul Anka's first No. 1 hit, "Lonely Boy." The song was criticized by the National Organization for Women, which awarded it their "Keep Her in Her Place" award. Critics said the song affirmed that the baby was the man's instead of the couple's.

"We tested the song before its release and knew there would be flak," Anka told the Los Angeles Times. "But it's nothing compared to the acceptance. I wasn't putting women in a subservient position, for God's sake. Motherhood is a fact of life."

Anka wrote "(You're) Having My Baby" for his wife and four daughters and recorded it as a duet with Odia Coates. Anka met the Oakland, CA, singer on tour, and the song became a duet on the suggestion of United Artists executive Bob Skaff.

Anka defended his song choice in a 1974 interview with Rolling Stone, saying, "It's not meant to alienate anyone. I could have called it 'having *our* baby,' but the other just sounded better. It's not a male ego trip—*my* baby.

"What I'm saying in the song is that there is a choice. The libbers will get on me; I can't help that. I *am* into the antihuman thing, and I *do* understand the other side of it.

"There are those who can't cope, and it's not in the cards for them to have kids. I'm a libber myself, in the sense that if you've got to abort, you do. Some people just can't cope."

Have you enjoyed 100 Greatest 70s Pop Songs? Then check out 100 Greatest 60s Pop Songs and the other music history books from Edgar Street Books!

About the Author

Frank Mastropolo is the author of Fillmore East: The Venue That Changed Rock Music Forever, chosen by Book Authority as one of the Best Classic Rock Music Books of All Time and by Best Classic Bands as one of the Best Music Books of the Year.

Mastropolo is a journalist, photographer, and former ABC News 20/20 writer and producer, winner of the Alfred I. DuPont–Columbia University silver baton and the Sigma Delta Chi award from the Society of Professional Journalists.

His work has appeared in Mojo, Classic Rock/Louder Sound, Relix, The Guardian, Untapped New York, and a variety of music and New York history sites. Mastropolo's rock concert photography is licensed by Getty Images and featured in the Bill Graham Rock & Roll Revolution museum exhibition.

For more information on our books and mini books, please visit Edgar Street Books.

Also by the Author

Fillmore East: The Venue That Changed Rock Music Forever
200 Greatest 60s Rock Songs, Vol. 1 and Vol. 2
200 Greatest 70s Rock Songs, Vol. 1 and Vol. 2
200 Greatest 80s Rock Songs
100 Greatest Soul Songs
100 Greatest 60s Pop Songs
100 Funniest Comedy Albums
New York Groove: An Inside Look at the Stars, Shows, and Songs That Make NYC Rock

Printed in Dunstable, United Kingdom

74527470R00070